a whole new you

THE MIRACULOUS CHANGE GOD HAS FOR YOUR LIFE

TONY EVANS

Multnomah Books

A WHOLE NEW YOU
published by Multnomah Books

©2006 by Tony Evans
International Standard Book Number 978-1-60142-406-8

Cover image by Steve Gardner, www.shootpw.com
Interior design and typeset by Katherine Lloyd, The DESK, Sisters, OR

Italics in Scripture references are the author's emphasis.
Unless otherwise indicated, Scripture quotations are from:
New American Standard Bible® (NASB) © 1960, 1977, 1995
by the Lockman Foundation. Used by permission.
Other Scripture quotations are from:
The Holy Bible, New International Version (NIV) © 1973, 1984
by International Bible Society, used by permission of Zondervan Publishing House
The Holy Bible, New King James Version (NKJV) © 1984 by Thomas Nelson, Inc.

Published in the United States by WaterBrook Multnomah, an imprint of the Crown
Publishing Group, a division of Random House Inc., New York.

MULTNOMAH and its mountain colophon are registered trademarks of Random House Inc.

For information:
MULTNOMAH BOOKS
12265 ORACLE BOULEVARD, SUITE 200 · COLORADO SPRINGS, CO 80921

Library of Congress Cataloging-in-Publication Data
Evans, Anthony T.
 A whole new you : the miraculous change God has for your life / Tony Evans.
   p. cm.
 ISBN 9781601424068
 1. Christian life. 2. Change (Psychology)--Religious aspects--Christianity. I. Title.
BV4509.5.E834 2006
248.4--DC22   2006010036

146655433

Contents

One

God's Assignment for Us

Is there anything more discouraging than to work hard at something and give it your best—only to realize in the end that all your efforts were in vain?

While I was in seminary preparing for the ministry, I was assigned to write a paper by a professor well-known for only rarely giving A's. I liked this kind of challenge, and I was committed to ace that paper no matter how much research it required or how many hours it took.

So I dug in and spared no effort. I clocked all-nighters, I did the research, I studied the original biblical languages. I wrote eighteen pages (though the professor only asked for ten or twelve), and carefully entered all the footnotes to cite my sources. I went the distance.

When I got my paper back, the letter *F* was marked on the front of it. Not only did I miss getting an A…I did not even make a B or C or D. You can imagine how crushed I felt.

I was thinking, *How dare he give me an F!* Then something caught my attention on the bottom of the page. It was a note the professor had written just below the grade mark: "Great scholarship, great detail, magnificent effort. But you answered the wrong question."

THE WRONG FOCUS

All that work addressing *the wrong thing*—the wrong assignment, the wrong purpose. My problem wasn't that I hadn't worked hard or wasn't sincere in what I'd written. The reason I missed out on what could have been a wonderful achievement was that, in my desire to score high, I was so focused on *me* and on what *I* wanted to achieve that I completely lost sight of what the professor actually wanted from me.

How closely does that picture apply to our Christian life?

Many of us are working hard at being a Christian. We're giving it overtime efforts—going to church, reading the Bible, saying our prayers, always trying to do better. We keep making promises to the Lord: We've committed our life, then recommitted it, and then recommitted the recommitment.

But it's not working. We still fail.

It's not that there's no sincerity; it's not that there's no trying; it's not that we aren't striving to be our best.

No, the real problem for so many of us is that we're so often focused on the wrong thing. We're missing what God is really looking for. So I want to help you understand what that is.

FINDING THE PURPOSE

We like to tell ourselves that God will work all things for good—an assumption we base on one of the greatest passages of the New Testament, where we find these words:

"We know that God causes all things to work together for good to those who love God, to those who are called according to His purpose" (Romans 8:28). But we tend to forget the last phrase in that verse—*called according to His purpose.* God is going to work all things for good only as those things fit with His purpose.

So when things in my life aren't coming together or working out for good—could the reason be that I haven't yet connected my life with His purpose? Maybe I'm still trying to get everything to work together for the good of *my* purpose.

So what *is* God's purpose for us?

God hasn't left us to guess the answer on our own. In the very next verse of that great New Testament passage, He clearly states His purpose for you and me: "For those whom He foreknew, He also predestined *to become conformed to the image of His Son,* so that He would be the firstborn among many brethren" (Romans 8:29).

God is telling us that He's looking for only one thing from you and me: that we be conformed to the image of His Son, Jesus Christ. That's His goal, the driving force that He wants behind our entire existence, and His only objective in knitting together all the details of our life.

It's also the only assignment God grades. It's the only direction He wants us going, and if you're not going there, you're just not on the same page with God. So if you're moving in any direction *other* than conformity to Christ—then don't expect the pieces of your life to make sense.

With God, this purpose is a *family* affair. God places a priority on reproducing His Son in a multitude of redeemed humanity, so that Christ will be "the firstborn among *many* brethren." God didn't want there to be only one Person who reflected His character—He wanted Jesus Christ to have a whole host of little brothers and little sisters who reflect their big Brother's character and goodness.

God the Father is so in love with His Son that He wants to make a whole community of people who look *just like Him*—so that when people see you and me, they'll get a glimpse of Jesus.

> The Father is so high on the Son that He wanted to give Him something. "What can I give My Son to let Him know how much I love Him? I'll give Him an entire race, a company of redeemed citizens!" So if you are saved, you are a gift from the Father to the Son. —❖•

JUST LIKE JESUS

Many people who have visited our home have marveled at something they see on a little table near the entry. It's a picture frame containing side-by-side photographs. On the right is a picture of me when I was eighteen; on the left is a picture of my son, Tony Jr., when he was eighteen. People are amazed by the close resemblance, and they say we look like twins. Why do we look so much alike? Because of a DNA connection. My essence has been transferred to my son, and in the process of his development, he winds up looking like me.

In the living body of Jesus Christ, we see a human being who perfectly contains all the DNA of deity. Over and over again the Bible assures us of this fact. Jesus is "the exact representation" of God's nature (Hebrews 1:3); "in Him all the fullness of Deity dwells in bodily form" (Colossians 2:9). Therefore Jesus "is the image of God" (2 Corinthians 4:4), "the image of the invisible God" (Colossians 1:15).

And now God wants to transfer that same divine DNA to a group or class of people called "Christians"—the redeemed community of saints, the elect of God, who are adopted into His family. They're the men and women and boys and girls who are committed to God's Son, Jesus Christ, and His divine DNA transfer is accomplished in them when they come to faith in Christ as their Savior. That's why Peter tells us that through God's promises we "may become partakers of the divine nature" (2 Peter 1:4).

"That's My purpose for you," God is telling us, "and it's My *only* purpose. And to accomplish this purpose, I'm going to take all the pieces of your lives—the good, the bad, and the ugly—and I'm going to orchestrate them together for good, for your maximum benefit and your abundant life."

Our problem—and the reason so many of us stay so defeated for so long—is that we've failed to grasp this purpose. We're working on the wrong assignment, writing the wrong paper. Because unless the priority of your life and my life is Christlikeness—being conformed to the image of Jesus Christ—you won't be able to recognize God working all this out. You won't be able to see it.

That's a great tragedy, because by coming to faith in the Lord Jesus as your Sin-Bearer, and by launching out into this destiny of conformity to Christ, you've gotten mixed up into something that's beyond your wildest dreams. You've been divinely called into a cosmic relationship with staggering implications.

We get a glimpse of it in John 17, in what's known as the "High Priestly Prayer" of Jesus. He prayed these words to His Father on the night before He died on the cross.

He said, "Father, the hour has come; glorify Your Son, that the Son may glorify You" (John 17:1). And again, "Father, glorify Me together with Yourself, with the glory which I had with You before the world was" (17:5). Jesus was essentially saying this: "Father, make Me look good so I can make You look good, and We'll make each other look good!"

This glory extends to you and me as well. Jesus prayed for His followers—all of us—and spoke these words: "The glory which You have given Me I have given to them" (17:22). And He prayed this: "Father, I desire that they also, whom You have given Me, be with Me where I am, so that they may see My glory which You have given Me" (17:24). He's including *us* in all this looking good! The Father and the Son were having so much fun, they wanted to share it. They wanted a company of redeemed humanity who could get in on all this.

You and I have gotten hooked up into the reality of the Father and the Son making each other look good, and Jesus makes it clear that He wants us to be a part of it. The Father is consumed with the Son, and the Son is consumed with the Father—and together, they want to let you and me get in on this interpersonal immersion.

It's all something bigger than you or I could ever

imagine, with eternal implications connected to it.

But here's the problem. If all this doesn't match our own priority, then we won't be hanging with the Father and the Son the way They intend for us to.

IT'S NOT ABOUT HAPPINESS

Let me say it again: God's purpose for you and me is Christlikeness, which means being conformed to the character of Christ. It's having God's values and God's conduct expressed in *your* humanity, through the uniqueness of *your* personality. *Christlikeness* simply means emulating who Christ is—not because you're stressing and straining, but because Christ is in you.

That means His purpose for you is *not* a great job, or your perfect health. His purpose for you is not that you have a wonderful family. Those are benefits—good benefits. And it's fine to want a good job and a nice family and good health. But none of those happen to be His major objective for you.

His purpose is not even your happiness. Am I suggesting that God wants you *un*happy? No. I'm suggesting that happiness is not His prevailing goal for you. Conforming you to His Son is what He's really after.

In Gethsemane, on the night He was betrayed, Jesus said to His Father, "My Father, if it is possible, let this cup pass from Me" (Matthew 26:39). It was like He was saying, "This cup of suffering is an unhappy position, and it's not where I'd rather be. But I'm not here for Me ('Not as I will…'); I'm here for *You* ('Your will be done' [v. 42])."

What I'm talking about here implies a radical departure from the way most of us look at our life. Most of us think that we are here on this earth for ourselves. Most of us spend our time wanting God to bless what *we're* about. God is not against blessing what we're about—as long as what we're about is what *He's* about, which is one thing only—conforming us to the image of His Son.

And when we conform to the Son, we also conform to the Father, because Jesus was perfectly conformed to God in heaven. According to John 14, they let us in on their relationship.

I like the twist we see in John 14:19-20. Jesus is helping

His disciples glimpse the new realities they'll enjoy after His resurrection, and He says, "Because I live, you will live also." Then He mentions three things that they will grasp and understand "in that day": "You will know that [1] I am in My Father, and [2] you in Me, and [3] I in you."

Imagine, if you will, a large envelope that represents God the Father. Then imagine another envelope inside the larger one. The inner envelope is His Son, Jesus Christ, and inside it are all those who follow Him. And that makes us feel good—it's a picture of security, because we're sealed (or marked that we belong to God) inside that envelope by the Spirit: It's by "the Holy Spirit of God" that we "were sealed for the day of redemption" (Ephesians 4:30).

But the picture doesn't end there. Jesus tells us in John 14:20 that not only is He in His Father, and not only are we in Jesus, but *Jesus is in us*. He doubles back on us!

When we read in the Bible how you and I are *in Christ*, that speaks of our secure relationship with the Lord that He gives us through our salvation. And when we read how *Christ is in us*, it leads us to God's whole purpose for our salvation, which is that Christ might express *His* life through *our* lives. He tells us, "You're not only in Me, but I am now in you."

If you take a poker and set it in a fireplace where a fire is raging, the poker will eventually become red-hot. It doesn't get that way because it *wants* to be red-hot or because it's in a hot mood or because it's trying so hard to heat up. It gets that way just because of where it's hanging out— because of its environment; it's *in the fire*. And because the poker's in the fire, the fire is now in the poker. If you take it out and reach over to touch the hot tip to a newspaper or a sofa pillow or the window curtains, you'll set them aflame.

So in your own life, if you're touching the people and situations around you, and nothing's burning, nothing's changing, no spiritual fires are starting… maybe it's because you haven't been fully in the fire. —:•

A PROBLEM OF CAPACITY

Suppose I had a genuine, heartfelt, passionate desire to be a great professional basketball player. More than anything else in the world, I wanted to play in the NBA on the same level as Michael Jordan.

Well, there are some obvious problems with that. First, there are physical limitations. I'm only six feet tall, and I'm too fat and slow. And I'm in my fifties, about thirty years too old to start a professional basketball career.

Furthermore, there's also the little problem of my lack of skills to play at that level.

So the problem with me being an NBA basketball star would not be a lack of desire or a lack of study, but a lack of capacity. Even if I read Michael Jordan's latest instructional book, I just don't have what it takes to pull off what he writes about. I can read it over and over, understand every word, and go out to my driveway and practice all day. But none of that changes the fact that I simply don't have the capacity to do what he did. And the harder I tried to play on his level, the more I would end up frustrated and discouraged.

Likewise, there are a lot of Christians who are frustrated and discouraged because they can't seem to pull off living the abundant life Jesus promised them. They can't seem to make themselves more like Jesus, no matter how hard they try. They've read all the fundamentals God has given them in the Bible, and they even do their best to put them into practice. But they just can't make it work.

In truth, there isn't one man or woman who has ever lived with the ability to be just like Jesus. There are a lot of frustrated and discouraged Christians today who have tried. They're reading their Bibles, but they're still addicted. They're praying every day, but they can't shake that sinful attitude or behavior. They're even trying to share their faith with others, but they don't see anyone coming to Christ.

Why are so many Christians living in defeat when Jesus promised them victory? Paul gives us a hint: "If Christ is in you, *though the body is dead because of sin*, yet the spirit is alive because of righteousness" (Romans 8:10).

You see, we've got a capacity problem: We live in mortal

physical bodies that are dead because of sin. Therefore we're no more able to be like Jesus than I'm able to play basketball like Michael. It doesn't matter how hard we try, how many New Year's resolutions we make, or how many promises or vows we utter, because we just don't have the capacity within us to do it. Sure, many of us have the ability to be "good people," and many of us will have some good days or weeks in doing many of the things God calls us to do. But in reality, we're still only corpses, because sin has killed our ability to be what God wants us to be.

That sounds like an impossible situation, doesn't it? Even though God says He wants to conform us to the image of His Son, none of us has the capacity to do it.

But our God loves working with the impossible, and He's made a way for you to become more and more like Jesus every day you walk with Him.

For me to play basketball like Michael Jordan would require something that's humanly impossible: Michael would have to take up residence inside me and empower my mind and body to do what I couldn't otherwise do.

With the spirit of Michael living in my body, I could shoot jumpers, throw down spectacular dunks, and hit my teammates with eye-popping passes. In biblical language, it would mean that I've become conformed to the image of Michael Jordan.

Of course, no human being can do that. But God *can!* Not only that, He has!

Too many of us take a backward approach when it comes to Christlikeness. We try to "fix" ourselves spiritually by "doing" the things we believe will make us better Christians. But that means we're trying to fix the problem with what *is* the problem in the first place: ourselves. It's like having your house destroyed by fire, then trying to rebuild it using only the ashes and charred remains. It's a case of something completely dead trying to raise itself back to life. I'm no medical expert, but I'm confident there has never been a case of someone actually dead who willed himself or herself back to life. Once they died, they stayed that way, no matter how much that person might have wanted to go on living.

The virus of sin has so infected the body that *you* cannot help *you*. The body is dead. That's why Paul says, "The good that I want, I do not do, but I practice the very evil that I do not want" (Romans 7:19). And he cries out, "Wretched man that I am! Who will set me free from the body of this death?" (Romans 7:24).

Paul is like us when we cry out, "I want to do right, but I can't. I want to get off drugs, or alcohol, but I can't. I want to stop sleeping around, but I can't. I want to stop looking at the pornographic Web sites, but I can't. I try. I make promises. I go to church. I go to Bible study. I really want to get out of this…but I can't."

It's true—*you* can't. Because the thing you're using to try and get out of it is dead. —:•

It's a hopeless situation. Hopeless, that is, until we read Paul's description of the greatest miracle of all time and what it means to us: "But if the Spirit of Him who raised Jesus from the dead dwells in you, He who raised Christ Jesus from the dead will also give life to your mortal bodies through His Spirit who dwells in you" (Romans 8:11).

Most Christians today see their faith in Jesus as a way to have forgiveness of sin and a place in God's eternal kingdom. But that's just the beginning. Paul is telling us that when we know Jesus Christ as our personal Lord and Savior, we have dwelling within us the very same Holy Spirit who raised Him from the dead two thousand years ago—and He will give *us* life also.

What a wonderful privilege it is to know that God Himself, in the form of the Holy Spirit, lives inside us. When you know Jesus and have His Holy Spirit living inside you, you're a candidate for a miracle, the miracle called *resurrection*. Although you were once spiritually dead and rotting, now you're made alive. You are, in the words of Jesus Himself, "born again" (John 3:3).

If you were to ask most believers what they want more than anything when it comes to their walk with

God, you might hear something like this: "I want to be a better person." While there's nothing necessarily wrong with wanting to be a better person, that's not why God sent Jesus to earth to live and die, then rise from the dead. He did those things so we could be *completely new people*. He doesn't want to simply improve what is dead; He wants to transform us and raise us from the dead. This is the heart of Christlikeness—the Spirit-inspired ability to increasingly imitate the character and conduct of Christ in and through our own bodies.

There truly is only one way to have victory, and this is it: To respond to God by making conformity to the image of Jesus Christ not just your number one priority in life, but your life's passion. When you do that, you're in position to experience that miracle called *resurrection*.

But the question remains: How exactly do we do this? How does it work? What, if anything, can we do to conform ourselves more and more fully to the image of Jesus?

Read on, and you'll find out!

Two

The Road to Transformation

B eing a father and a grandfather, I have had several opportunities to witness the transformation that takes place in a woman's body as she progresses through pregnancy and on to childbirth. And if there's one thing I've learned about pregnancy, it's this: The changes don't take place because of any effort on the part of the woman or on the part of the growing baby inside her.

The mother doesn't just say to herself, "I think I'm going to start showing today so everyone knows I'm pregnant. And I'll do that by nourishing my baby through the umbilical cord so that he grows bigger." She also doesn't just decide to change her appetite for the things that are

25

best for the baby or to start producing milk to nourish her infant.

If you've taken even the most rudimentary biology class, you know that a baby's development is not a matter of effort but of nature. When a woman becomes pregnant, her body changes from the inside out as the baby inside her naturally starts growing and developing to the point where you can't help but see that she's expecting.

This miraculous process of conception and growth illustrates how our transformation to Christlikeness is supposed to work, and that's apart from anything we as believers "do" to make it happen.

A (SUPER)NATURAL TRANSFORMATION

God wants your transformation to Christlikeness to happen apart from any independent personal "effort" on your part, other than to commit yourself to allowing Him to make the necessary changes from the inside out. He doesn't want you to strive or to try to be a "better Christian." He doesn't want you to "will" yourself into growing and becoming the whole new you He promised you would be.

God wants people to see the glow of His presence shining out from within us, much as it did for Moses when he returned from a mountaintop experience with God: "It came about when Moses was coming down from Mount Sinai (and the two tablets of the testimony were in Moses' hand as he was coming down from the mountain), that Moses did not know that the skin of his face shone because of his speaking with Him. So when Aaron and all the sons of Israel saw Moses, behold, the skin of his face shone, and they were afraid to come near him" (Exodus 34:29–30).

Moses hadn't done anything to make his face shine for everyone to see; in fact, he didn't even realize he was shining at all. Moses had simply submitted himself to being in God's presence, and what that had done within him shone out from inside. It was the natural result of a supernatural experience.

God wants the very same thing to happen to us.

> The pressing question is this: How do I experience *naturally* this transformation that God talks about? How do I experience it in reality? How does it just "flow"? —:•

But the question for each and every one of us is, If God doesn't want us striving and straining toward Christlikeness, then how can we be transformed? In one of my favorite passages of Scripture, the apostle Paul gives us some key elements of true spiritual transformation: "Now the Lord is the Spirit, and where the Spirit of the Lord is, there is liberty. But we all, with unveiled face, beholding as in a mirror the glory of the Lord, are being transformed into the same image from glory to glory, just as from the Lord, the Spirit" (2 Corinthians 3:17–18).

The first thing we need to notice about this passage is the One who is responsible for our transformation—God's own Holy Spirit.

THE AGENT OF TRANSFORMATION

Paul begins 2 Corinthians 3:17 by telling his readers, "Now the Lord is the Spirit." That tells us something we all need to remember as we seek to be transformed: The Holy Spirit is God. Though He plays a role in our lives different from that of the Father or the Son, He possesses every attribute of God.

A short time before He went to the cross, Jesus promised His disciples, "I will ask the Father, and He will give you another Helper, that He may be with you forever; that is the Spirit of truth, whom the world cannot receive, because it does not see Him or know Him, but you know Him because He abides with you and will be in you" (John 14:16–17).

A lot of struggling believers are just sure that if Jesus were only with them physically, they could do better when it comes to living the Christian life. But the Bible contains the accounts of twelve individuals who walked with, talked with, ate with, and learned from Jesus day after day for over three years. And how did they do? If you read through the gospels, you'll see that they argued with one another, they doubted Jesus and completely missed out on much of what He taught them, and, at the very moment of truth, they abandoned Him as He took those final steps to the cross.

That doesn't sound like a group of men who had been transformed, does it?

Jesus had chosen His disciples for the specific purpose of taking His message of salvation to the world around them. But for that to happen, they were each going to have to undergo a spiritual transformation. They were going to have to be made into new men, a process Jesus started by teaching them daily through His words and deeds and through testing them in their faith, encouraging them, and even chiding them when they needed it.

But Jesus knew from the very beginning that the process of transforming these men—all of them ordinary, average fellows with the same human weaknesses each of us has—wasn't going to be complete until they received the gift of the Holy Spirit, an event that wasn't going to happen until after His death and resurrection.

When Jesus appeared to the disciples following His death and resurrection, He made good on His promise of a Helper: "So Jesus said to them again, 'Peace be with you; as the Father has sent Me, I also send you.' And when He had said this, He breathed on them and said to them, 'Receive the Holy Spirit'" (John 20:21–22).

Now, having received the Holy Spirit, the disciples' transformation was complete. They had learned the Word of God and how to apply it from their Master, and now they had received the empowerment He had promised them in the person of God's own Spirit. They were ready to go out and make a difference in the world around them and do it as completely transformed men.

We need to understand what the disciples understood once they received the Holy Spirit: When we have God's Spirit inside us, we don't have to wonder how much better we would be doing in our walks with Jesus if He were only with us. That's because He *is* with us—in the person of the Holy Spirit—teaching us, convicting us, instructing us, empowering us…transforming us.

The Bible tells us that "where the Spirit of the Lord is,

there is liberty." Another word for "liberty" in this context is "freedom." That means that when we are in tune with God's Holy Spirit, we are freed from being what we once were and freed to be what God intends for us to be: reflections of Jesus Christ.

God wants us to understand that there will be transformation taking place anywhere His Spirit is. That means that all things are new for the believer, and that includes the way we think and the way we view the world and our place in it.

A NEW WAY OF THINKING

Paul wrote to the first-century Roman believers, "For those who are according to the flesh set their minds on the things of the flesh, but those who are according to the Spirit, the things of the Spirit. For the mind set on the flesh is death, but the mind set on the Spirit is life and peace" (Romans 8:5–6).

This tells us that it is vitally important as we are being conformed to the image of Christ that we make the Holy

Spirit's way of thinking our way of thinking. And what is the Holy Spirit's way of thinking? It's the same thinking as God the Father. It means understanding and operating based on God's point of view.

Christlikeness isn't just behaving like Christ, it's also thinking like Christ. It is having what the Bible calls "the mind of Christ" (1 Corinthians 2:16). And if you want to see what the mind of Christ really is, you need only look at the things He did and said during His earthly ministry.

Jesus lived a perfectly sinless life because His mind was constantly filled with nothing but the thoughts of God. He was mentally focused on being in perfect obedience to the Father in every detail of His life. This is why He was able to repel the devil's efforts to tempt Him into abandoning His earthly calling (see Matthew 4:1–11), why He was able to live a life of perfect service to God and His disciples, and why He was able to obey His Father to the point of giving Himself up to die a horrible, gruesome death on the cross.

Though it is completely contrary to our sinful flesh, we as believers are called to think exactly as Jesus thought and still thinks.

The Bible tells us that as a man "thinks within himself, so he is" (Proverbs 23:7). This has meaning far beyond what we have heard called "the power of positive thinking." In a spiritual sense, this means that the things we focus our minds upon not only influence what we do but actually become part of who we are.

Whenever we find ourselves not living right, we can always look back and see that the things we are doing are rooted in the way we have been thinking. No one who falls into sin can honestly say "It just happened." If someone enters into an adulterous or sexually immoral relationship, it is for one of two reasons. Either that person entertained in his or her mind the idea of taking part in that kind of behavior, or that person didn't make God's thinking about that kind of sin his or her own thinking.

One biblical example of this truth can be found in 2 Samuel 11, where we read of King David's thinking before he fell into sin with Bathsheba. This passage tells us, "Now when evening came David arose from his bed and walked around on the roof of the king's house, and from the roof he saw a woman bathing; and the woman was very beautiful in appearance" (v. 2).

We don't have to read too far between the lines of that verse to see that David had allowed wrong thinking to enter his head when it came to Bathsheba. He watched her bathing and could see that she was pleasing to the eye. From there, that seed of lust grew into actions that would change forever the course of David's life—and the lives of many others, including his faithful servant Uriah, who lost his life as a result of David's sin. (See 2 Samuel 11:3-17.)

Many Christians can't live according to the Spirit because they think toward the flesh. That is why so many believers are still in bondage to the things of the flesh, even though they may truly desire the freedom we are promised in Jesus Christ.

What do we need to do in order to have our thinking— and therefore, everything else about us—transformed? There is a hint in 2 Corinthians 3:18, and it's as simple is changing the way we look at God and how we allow Him to look at us.

A NEW WAY OF "LOOKING" AT GOD

The Bible tells us that in order to be transformed into the image of Christ, we have to remove all hindrances that keep us from seeing God as He is and ourselves as we are. Paul put it this way: "But we all, with unveiled face, beholding as in a mirror the glory of the Lord" (2 Corinthians 3:18).

That sounds a bit on the mysterious side, doesn't it? But what Paul is telling us is that when we come to God, we must not just look at Him but gaze at Him intently. We'll see how to do that in a moment, but he's also telling us that we must allow Him to see us as we are, hiding nothing. To put it in more modern terms, we must be willing to be completely and totally vulnerable with God, keeping nothing hidden from Him.

In a traditional wedding, the bride walks down the aisle to her groom wearing a veil that obscures her face. But as the groom lifts the veil over his beloved's face to kiss her, her face is fully visible to him. That is exactly how God wants us to allow Him to see us as we approach Him. In fact, if you want to be transformed to the image of Jesus Christ, it is an absolute necessity.

That is exactly what the Bible tells us Moses did when he approached God: "But whenever Moses went in before the LORD to speak with Him, he would take off the veil until he came out" (Exodus 34:34). Moses didn't settle for letting God see his face obscured through a veil, but instead, allowed Him to see his face fully—to see him for who and what he really was. He was fully exposed before God.

Before you can be who and what you want to be in Christ, you must be willing to be fully exposed and fully honest before God about who and what you are right now. You can't come to Him talking, thinking, and acting like everything is right when it isn't. You can't come to Him with fake prayers and fake spirituality. You have to be real with Him.

KEEPING IT REAL WITH GOD

I've talked with many believers who come to me and say, "Pastor, my prayers seem stale. It seems like I'm saying the same things over and over and nothing is happening."

When I hear that, I suggest that the reason that person is saying the same things to God over and over is because there are things he or she doesn't want to talk to Him about.

Instead of getting down with what's really going on in their lives, many believers come to God spouting what I call "canned prayers." All they talk to God about is how they want to be blessed, and they do that without dealing with what's really on their hearts and, more importantly, on God's heart.

In other words, they are hiding from God because they are coming to Him with a veil over their face.

Nothing about those kinds of prayers has anything to do with our being transformed and conformed to the image of Jesus Christ. On the other hand, coming to God being completely open and honest about the things you know are not Christlike—that's the kind of prayers that move you closer to truly being the new you.

We all need to understand that there is no place we can go and nothing we can do to hide ourselves from God. King David wrote and rhetorically asked, "Where can I go from Your Spirit? Or where can I flee from Your presence? If I ascend to heaven, You are there; If I make my bed in Sheol, behold, You are there" (Psalm 139:7–8).

This means that God already knows everything about you. He knows about all your sin and shortcomings. He knows about the addictions, habits, behaviors, thought patterns, and attitudes that keep you from enjoying intimate fellowship with Him. He knows those things, and He wants more than anything for you to bring them to Him openly and honestly so that He can deal with them.

A lot of Christians, however, make the mistake of offering "blanket prayers" when it comes to their sin. They pray something like, "Lord, forgive me for all the sins I have committed today." But that's not exposure. That is hiding in your darkness by using what you think are the right words. That's like going to your doctor and just telling him, "Do something about my pain" without telling him where it hurts. Just as you'd leave a doctor's appointment like that one still sick and hurting, you leave a session of "blanket confession" still in bondage and darkness.

God is not interested in hearing our "cutesy" blanket prayers. He's only interested in us doing as Moses did and going to Him with an uncovered face, hiding nothing and exposing everything. He's only interested in us taking to Him the things that keep us from being like Jesus Christ and allowing Him to change those things and transform us. He's only interested in our giving the Holy Spirit permission to change what needs to be changed, remove what needs to be removed, and install what needs to be installed in our lives to make us more like Jesus.

The problem with many Christians is that they are glancers, not beholders. They don't bother to take the veils off their faces and gaze intently at the Lord, but instead, settle for quick glances available to anyone who cares to take a peek. But there is no way that we will be "transformed from glory to glory" if we don't remove the veils from our faces and truly behold the glory of God and allow Him to see the real us.

That is the way God set up the process of transformation "from glory to glory." And it's the only way we can do it and hope for it to be any kind of "natural" process.

DOING WHAT'S NATURAL

If you've ever needed to lose some weight and gone on any kind of diet, you know it can be a miserable experience. There are countless diets out there now—low-fat diets, low-carb diets, liquid diets, milkshake diets…the list goes on and on. But if there's one thing all these diets have in common (other than being miserable experiences for most of us), it's this: They just aren't natural.

It's not natural to walk around miserable because you can't eat, because certain foods aren't "allowed" in your diet. It's not natural to see other folks enjoying good food and say to yourself, "I can't eat that! I can't… I can't…I can't." And because it's not natural, our efforts to lose a few pounds are more often than not met with discouragement and frustration. Even if we lose some weight, we become so miserable and frustrated that we give up…and probably gain the weight back within a few weeks.

The 'Holy Spirit is like a fitness trainer in a gym whose job is to transform your spiritual flab into muscle. He has helped many a person before, and now He can help you. He knows fully how you're put together, and He knows the best personal program for getting you into shape. —:•

Nowadays, nutritionists and trainers will tell you that the best way to lose weight and get in shape is to do it naturally, meaning through making healthy eating and consistent exercise part of our lifestyle. For many of us, that means a whole new approach to life. But after we make those things part of our lives, they become second nature to us, part of how we just naturally live. We come to a point where we actually enjoy eating right and exercising, simply because we see the positive changes in how we look and how we feel. Then, it is no longer a matter of trying or striving to lose weight and get healthy. It just becomes part of who we are— the "new us."

When it comes to making changes in our physical bodies, going natural is always the best way. The very same thing is true in the spiritual realm. God never intended for us to try to change ourselves, and He certainly never meant for us to strive and fuss to change others—our spouses, our children, and our friends included. When we try to change ourselves or others through our own fleshly efforts, there is sure to be conflict and misery. That's because it's not natural, not God's will for us to do it that way.

There is only one way to effectively and genuinely change ourselves, and it's to get ourselves in front of God and let Him see us as we really are—all of us, and not just those parts we are comfortable letting Him see—then we will be transformed into what He wants us to be. God wants us to know that His Agent of Change, the Holy Spirit, is more than powerful enough to change anyone—to make them a new man or woman—if we but take the time to become beholders, when we focus our attention on Him.

TRANSFORMED BY GAZING

The Gospel of Luke contains a wonderful example of transformation through gazing. It occurred after Jesus' resurrection, and it happened to two men who had no idea what was happening to them until after it was finished.

The twenty-fourth chapter of Dr. Luke's gospel tells us that two of Jesus' followers—both of them seriously down in the dumps because their Master had died—were on the road about seven miles from Jerusalem, on their way to a place called Emmaus. But into the depths of their disappointment and despair stepped a Stranger who shared with them more information about what had happened to Jesus than they had any reason to expect that day.

As they walked along talking about what had happened during the previous few days, Jesus Himself sidled up to them and began walking with them. At that point in the story, neither of them had any idea who this Stranger was because, as Luke tells us, "they were kept from recognizing him" (Luke 24:16 NIV). Jesus' true identity was veiled from them.

"What are you discussing together?" Jesus asked them, then listened as they recounted how the Man named Jesus of Nazareth, a Prophet who knew and taught the Word of God like no one they had ever heard and who performed incredible miracles, had been arrested, taken to the authorities, then crucified. They were bitterly disappointed because they had believed He was the One who was going to deliver Israel once and for all. Now He was dead, and they were on their way back home, where they would continue living the same lives they had lived before.

At this point, Jesus could have just stopped, thrown off the veil that kept these men from recognizing Him, and said, "I'm here! I've risen from the dead. I really am everything you thought I was when I walked with you and talked with you every day!" But He didn't do that. Jesus had something more to teach these boys.

Still walking on the road to Emmaus with these two disciples, Jesus began teaching them. "How foolish you are, and how slow of heart to believe all the prophets have spoken!" He said to them. "Did not the Christ have to suffer these things and then enter his glory?" (Luke 24:25–26 NIV). Jesus then went on to remind them, starting with the books of Moses and then all the Old Testament prophets, that everything that had happened to Him had been in exact accordance to the promises God had given the Jewish people concerning the Messiah many centuries before.

These two fellahs could tell that this Stranger who walked with them knew His Bible. He taught them like no one had ever taught them—other than Jesus Himself that is. Still, they didn't know who He was.

That revelation wouldn't happen until they arrived at their homes. Jesus walked along with them until they reached their homes, and once they arrived there, Jesus acted as if He was going to continue on. But these men wanted to see more and hear more of this Man who seemed to have such amazing understanding. In true Jewish hospitality, they invited Him in.

That night, as they began breaking bread together, the veil came off their eyes, and something happened. They saw Jesus. They saw the very same God-Man they had known for so long as their Teacher and miracle worker. But this time it was different. This time it was the Jesus who had died on their behalf but who had also defeated death. It was the Jesus who was preparing to return home to His Father.

These men had done something that was completely natural when Jesus was with them: They gazed at Him. And because they did that, He revealed Himself to them. After that, their lives would never be the same.

God has saved each and every one of us so that we could be conformed to the image of His Son. But too many of us are striving and working to make it happen, only to find ourselves discouraged and frustrated. God wants us to rely on His Holy Spirit to transform us as we gaze into His face and see Him as He really is and allow Him to see us as we really are. When we do that, we will be transformed into His image "from glory to glory."

Glory to glory. I've always loved that term. When I read it, I think of the transformation a wriggly little caterpillar undergoes as he spins himself into a cocoon, where he is transformed into a beautiful butterfly. More importantly, I think of the transformation Jesus wants to do in all of us, first by gloriously giving us the rebirth we all need in order to see His kingdom. But it doesn't stop there. As we make the decision to continually gaze into His face, God, through His Holy Spirit, continually transforms us from one level of transformation to another, each of which results in us being more like Jesus than we were before. It's that wonderful process of making us new people as He conforms us to the image of His Son, Jesus Christ.

Three

Transformed by the Word

In the last chapter, we talked about God's Agent of transformation: the Holy Spirit. Any agent needs tools or instruments to do their work, and God has one in His written Word, the Bible.

Sadly, too many believers today are suffering from what I call "spiritual anorexia." God has given them all the "food" they could ever need through His Word, yet they refuse to eat, leaving them powerless, defeated, and without hope. They're fighting sin and losing. Fighting addictions and losing. Fighting sinful thought patterns and attitudes and losing.

You don't have to be a Bible scholar to know that God's

written Word promises us that we will be changed, even transformed, when we place our faith in Jesus Christ. But how does this work? What can we do to make ourselves more like Jesus as we read His Word?

The apostle Paul gives us a hint in a verse we looked at earlier when he writes, "But we all, with unveiled face, beholding as in a mirror the glory of the Lord, are being transformed into the same image from glory to glory, just as from the Lord, the Spirit" (2 Corinthians 3:18).

At a glance, this still sounds a little mysterious, doesn't it? When Paul tells us that "we all, with unveiled face, beholding as in a mirror the glory of the Lord," he is talking about one thing: the Word of God. He wants us to understand that if we want to be transformed, we need to look at the standard for life and faith and the absolute truth God has given us in His written Word.

When you gaze into the Bible, Paul is telling us, you are to do so as though you were looking into a mirror. But this is not a mirror that reflects your own image back to you, but one that reflects back to you the glory of God in the person of Jesus Christ. The Bible is only beneficial to you when you look at it as a reflection of Jesus Christ, the One about whom the entire Bible—from the first word of Genesis to the last word in Revelation—was written.

> Jesus Christ is inviting you to get dressed spiritually in front of His mirror—the mirror of His Word, the mirror of His transformation, the mirror that reveals all. So come to Him with no camouflages, no hidden agendas, no acting like it's okay when it's not. Confess your sin, bring your sin before Him, and call it what He calls it. His Holy Spirit will expose you…so you can receive God's forgiveness and move forward into His transformation. —∗

There is no way we can properly look into God's Word and not be changed. But how do we do that? If, on the other hand, we continue to fight a losing battle against addictions, sinful habits, and ungodly thought patterns, then it's not a problem of trying harder or wanting to change. It is, in fact, a mirror problem.

How can we learn to truly behold God's Word and not just glance at it?

LEARNING TO "BEHOLD" GOD'S WORD

So many Christians today spend countless hours reading their Bibles, yet there is something missing. They learn a lot about what the Bible has to say and they may even apply some of it to their lives, but when it comes right down to it, they haven't been transformed by what they've read.

I believe one of the reasons that these believers aren't transformed by God's Word is that they miss out on one key word Paul used in 2 Corinthians 3:18, namely the word *beholding*. God doesn't want us just to look at His Word and then walk away. He wants us to "behold it," meaning look at it intently. That's because it is in His Word that we see a reflection of His true glory and character, and it's where we see the face of Jesus Christ.

But what must we do in order for that to happen? How can we be truly transformed by God's Word and not just enlightened or educated? The apostle James gave us some excellent and very practical directions for beholding the Word of God in the first chapter of his epistle.

This incredible Scripture passage contains some essentials when it comes to transformation through the Word of God, the first being one that seems fairly obvious but is difficult for far too many believers: listening to what God has to say through His written Word.

TIME TO LISTEN UP!

We live in a time when listening has become a lost art. It seems that people are more interested in speaking their minds and asserting their right to be heard than they are in hearing what another has to say.

But the Bible tells us that listening is an absolute must for the Christian who wants to be transformed and conformed to the image of Jesus Christ. James tells us, "But everyone must be quick to hear, slow to speak and slow

to anger; for the anger of man does not achieve the right-eousness of God" (1:19–20). While that's good advice for anyone to follow in any human relationship, James is speaking specifically about listening to the Word of God.

Sadly, most Christians tend to speak first, and when they do listen, it's to everything but the Word of God. Only after they've exhausted every other option do they stick their noses in their Bible and find out what God has to say. But God wants us to do exactly the opposite. Instead of looking to human wisdom first, He wants us to be resigned to the truth of His Word, meaning that we accept it as the only absolute truth we turn to when we are seeking answers.

Christians cannot be truly transformed when they're either too busy listening to themselves or listening to other folks talking. I've met with many struggling believers who tell me what their friends have told them, what their families have told them, or what their counselors have told them about their situations. They're quick to talk and quick to listen to human reasoning and wisdom (as limited as that is), but far too slow to listen to what God has to say.

The apostle Peter wrote, "like newborn babies, long for the pure milk of the word, so that by it you may grow in respect to salvation" (1 Peter 2:2). This is a beautiful word picture of how we are to desire God's Word. If you've ever seen a baby nursing, you know that no one had to teach the baby to crave its mother's milk. It is an instinctive hunger built into the baby that drives him or her to nurse.

But there is another point we need to take away from this verse. In this context, the word *pure* refers to completely undiluted. In other words, he is telling us, we as believers need to have a hunger for the absolutely uncontaminated Word of God. We need a craving for the Word of God alone.

Unfortunately, people throughout the centuries have attempted to dilute the Word of God. They water it down, mix it in with human philosophy and reasoning, leaving a final product that doesn't have the power to change and transform believers. While good Bible-based teaching can be beneficial, there is nothing more important when it comes to spiritual nourishment of the believer than the Word of God itself.

Those of us who have eaten candied apples know that they can be a delicious treat. But what may not have crossed our minds as we've eaten them is that coating a pure, healthy fruit such as an apple actually dilutes or even counteracts the health benefits we receive from the apple itself. That's because you've added what we all know is an unhealthy food—white sugar—to something God provided in the natural to nourish us.

That is exactly what happens on a spiritual level when we dilute the goodness of God's Word. When we allow human opinions and input to water down the purity of what God has said to us in the Bible, we are in danger of counteracting or negating what He has to say to us.

If we want God to completely change and transform us, we must be committed to the truth of the Scriptures. We must resign ourselves to every word of what He has to say through the written Word.

READ, BUT LOSE THE ANGER FIRST

I can't speak for other people, but I remember well what would happen when I threw a temper tantrum as a child. It didn't help me get what I wanted, but only made things worse for me. My mother would tell me, "If you don't stop this crying, I'm going to give you something to cry about!" I knew then not only that I'd better shape up but also that my crying and throwing a fit wasn't going to help me get my way.

Nothing good comes to the life of a believer by getting angry with God over the things that are going on in your life. In fact, that is a sure way to get stuck right where you are. That's because God wants us to be humble and to listen to Him as He speaks through the Word, and because He wants to bring to fruition His righteous plans for us.

When we fuss and cry at God over what is going on in our lives, we can't hear Him above all the noise we're making. That's why it's important that in all situations we remain calm and settled and committed to hearing Him.

When we do that, then we are ready to take the step of actually receiving God's Word.

RECEIVING THE WORD

The writer of the epistle to the Hebrews tell us that the Word of God is "living and active and sharper than any two-edged sword, and piercing as far as the division of soul and spirit, of both joints and marrow, and able to judge the thoughts and intentions of the heart" (Hebrews 4:12).

In other words, the Word is powerful when it comes to showing us where and how to change and in giving us the power to be transformed. But we need to understand that reading the Bible, and even memorizing and understanding it to a point, won't do us a bit of good unless we receive it and receive it God's way.

That is what James was talking about when he wrote, "Therefore, putting aside all filthiness and all that remains of wickedness, in humility *receive the word implanted*, which is able to save your souls" (1:21).

Before we knew Jesus, our hearts were completely unable to receive His Word implanted. But when God saves us, He implants His truth and His reality inside us. That truth overwhelms the darkness that was once in our hearts, allowing Him, through His Holy Spirit, to transform us.

In this context, the word *implanted* refers to something that has been placed inside you, much as a doctor might give you an implant to help you overcome some physical difficulty. But this is a spiritual implant. It's a whole new nature—the nature of Jesus Christ—implanted inside you. This means that when you accept Jesus Christ as your personal Lord and Savior, the reality of the light of God is implanted within you. It's not just planted in your body or in your mind, but in the deepest part of you, where it transforms you body, mind, and spirit into the image of Jesus.

"Receive the word implanted," James says, and that word *receive* refers to *welcome*. Welcome the word implanted! Because all the potential of everything you will ever be spiritually is already inside you! —•

RECEIVING WITH A READY HEART

We just saw that James 1:21 tells us there is one step we must take in order to receive the Word of God, and it's this: "Therefore, putting aside all filthiness and all that remains of wickedness." In other words, when we go to the Word, we've got to first agree with God when it comes to what the Book says about us and our sin.

Believers who want to be truly transformed need to understand that the Word of God will not penetrate a heart that is harboring sin. If we refuse to bring our sin before God and lay it out for Him to see and deal with, there is no Bible reading, no sermon, and no counseling that can penetrate our hearts and move us toward transformation.

That is exactly the message God had for His people during the time of the prophet Hosea, who ministered to the kingdom of Israel during the second half of the eighth century BC God wanted to bless His people, but before He would do that, they would have to address the sin that had implanted itself within them: "Sow for yourselves righteousness, reap the fruit of unfailing love, and break up your unplowed ground; for it is time to seek the LORD, until he comes and showers righteousness on you. But you have planted wickedness, you have reaped evil, you have eaten the fruit of deception.

Because you have depended on your own strength and on your many warriors" (Hosea 10:12–13 NIV).

The Word of God won't penetrate our lives and our hearts when there is unaddressed sin in our lives. Sin blocks our fellowship with a holy God, leaving us in darkness. When we approach God and His Word that way, nothing is going to happen because the soil of our hearts is not ready or able to have it implanted in our hearts and minds.

Now you may be asking, "If the Word cannot bring about changes in my life because of sin, then what hope is there for my being transformed?" I would answer by pointing out that if we had to wait until we were sinless and perfect before we went to the Word, then none of us could go in the first place, even for salvation.

A lot of believers go to the Word of God because of some sin they can't beat or problem they can't fix, and that's a good thing to do, as long as they lay their sin out before God so that He can give them forgiveness and victory. The problem comes when we try to go to the Word while harboring or protecting our own "pet sins."

None of us is perfect when we come to the Word of

God. We are sinful creatures by nature, and nothing short of an act of God Himself can change the fact that we are lost in and enslaved to sin. But what we can do is come to God and lay out before Him our imperfections and allow Him to deal with them.

John tells us, "If we confess our sins, [God] is faithful and righteous to forgive us our sins and to cleanse us from all unrighteousness" (1 John 1:9). Only God can forgive our sins. Our part in that equation is one thing: confession. That means bringing all our sins to Him with a heart that says, "Lord, I want to be cleansed and freed from this sin, and I want You to cleanse me and forgive me."

RECEIVING GOD'S WORD IN HUMILITY

James tells us that the Word implanted in you is able to save your soul. It can deliver you, transform you, and change you from what you once were into something you could never be on your own. But James also says that in order to have the Word implanted in you, you must come to God "in humility." That literally means to come under the authority of the Word of God.

When we humble ourselves and bring ourselves under someone's authority, we put ourselves below them, submit ourselves to them, and allow them to direct and guide us from a position of superiority. We trust and respect that person enough to tell them, "What you say, I will do."

There are many examples in the Bible of people putting themselves under the authority of another. But there is no better example of what it means to put one's self under the authority of someone else than that of Jesus, who while He ministered on earth was completely and solidly submitted to the will of the Father.

Jesus came to earth, died on the cross, and sent the Holy Spirit so that we could be transformed, so that we could become something we weren't before. But that could only have happened if He was completely submitted to everything God the Father told Him to do.

The Word implanted in you can deliver you from addictions. It can deliver you from a life that isn't functioning as it should. It can deliver you from defeat. It can deliver you from a hurting and miserable marriage and make that relationship what God intended it to be. It can deliver you from the anger, the lust, the jealousy, and the frustration you just can't seem to shake.

But that will happen only when you submit yourself to the Word's authority, when you make it your standard for everything you do and think.

THE IMPORTANCE OF "DOING"

One of the greatest flaws in the Christian faith as it is practiced today is that we've somehow come to believe that exposure to the Word is enough to change us. But I can tell you with absolute certainty that you can go to church and hear the best preaching every time the doors are open, read the Bible your every waking hour, go to the best Bible college and seminary and still be no better off for it. You can read every Christian book published and listen to every Christian television and radio program on the air and still be basically unchanged. Sure, you might be able to quote Scripture by letter and verse with the best of them, but you'll still be the same as you were before you began doing all those things.

Hear this and take it to heart: Exposure alone to the Word won't change you! It won't make you any more transformed or any more the "whole new you" than exposure to the best exercise equipment around will transform or change your body. Just as having your body transformed through exercise equipment requires you to get on board and start moving and sweating, transformation through the Word of God requires you to respond and take some action.

That is what the Bible means when it says, "But prove yourselves doers of the word, and not merely hearers who delude themselves. For if anyone is a hearer of the word and not a doer, he is like a man who looks at his natural face in a mirror; for once he has looked at himself and gone away, he has immediately forgotten what kind of person he was" (James 1:22–24).

In the original language of James's epistle, the word for "hearer" can be translated into the word *auditor*. It has the same meaning as when a college student audits a class. In that case, the student attends classes, takes notes, and acquires information but doesn't take tests, write papers, or receive a grade or class credit. He or she is there for the sole purpose of acquiring knowledge. The person who audits a class attains some head knowledge, but he or she isn't closer to accomplishing what all college students enroll for in the first place: earning a diploma.

Simply hearing the Word—through reading or listening to others quote Scripture—won't bring about transformation if we don't act on what we've heard. Transformation happens when we read the Bible, ask God "What do I do with what I've just read?" then do it. When we don't approach the Word that way, we have made our "hearing" a waste of time and energy. That, James tells us, is self-delusion.

When God gave us His Word, He didn't do it so that we could just hear Him then go our merry way. God wants us to hear His Word then act on what we hear. That is obedience, and it's the only way we can be truly transformed into the image of Jesus Christ.

It's the Holy Spirit's job to take over in our lives and conform us to the image of Jesus Christ. Our part in that equation is to make sure we act on what we've heard when it comes to the Word of God. The Holy Spirit will be there to empower and enable the decision to obey...but won't make the decision for you.

SEEING YOURSELF IN THE MIRROR OF SCRIPTURE

Mirrors as we know them today—ones made of glass that can reflect our images back to us nearly perfectly—didn't come into existence until the fourteenth century. Prior to that, mirrors were made of shiny metal. The problem with those kinds of mirrors was that you couldn't get a clear, unobscured picture of yourself in them. People had to move the metallic mirrors around until the light was just right to give them a clearer view of themselves.

When James says "one who looks intently at the perfect law [the Word of God]" (1:25), he is suggesting with the word *intently* that we look at the Word—that we twist it, turn it, and gaze at it from different angles. I'm not talking about changing what God has said, and I'm not talking about making it "user friendly" so that it says what we want it to say. I'm talking about moving ourselves around so that we see the whole truth God wants us to see.

In the Bible, when you read of folks looking at the Word of God, they never do it apart from prayer and meditation. That's because they aren't just trying to enjoy some good reading but also are trying to look intently into the mirror of God's Word. They are coming to God and saying, "I want You to show me something about myself, but even more than that, I want You to show me something about You."

That is what King David was talking about when he wrote, "Open my eyes, that I may behold wonderful things from Your law" (Psalm 119:18); that is why the psalmist observed, "How blessed is the man who does not walk in the counsel of the wicked, nor stand in the path of sinners, nor sit in the seat of scoffers! But his delight is in the law of the LORD, and in His law he meditates day and night" (Psalm 1:1–2).

Notice that there is blessing in gazing intently on the Word of God. In both psalms, we see that just beholding is a blessing in and of itself. But there is more. When we focus our attention on God's Word, we are changed from the inside out. As we look at ourselves in the mirror of God's Word, we see ourselves in light of His standards, and we can't help but be changed.

When we look at God's Word, we must look intently, not just glance at it and look away. To do that is to walk away from the mirror unchallenged and unchanged. It would do us about as much good as going to a doctor, getting an X-ray, and then having the doctor glance at it and tell us everything was fine. In order for a doctor to know that there's nothing wrong with us, he has to gaze at the X-ray and look at all the details, making sure that everything is where it's supposed to be…and that nothing is there that shouldn't be.

God's Word gives us an inside-out look at who and what we really are. But that only happens as we look at it intently, meditate (or think) on it, and dwell in the truth and goodness of God and what He has to say about us. That is what James was talking about when he wrote, "But one who looks intently at the perfect law, the law of liberty, and abides by it, not having become a forgetful hearer but an effectual doer, this man will be blessed in what he does" (1:25).

When you discover that God's Word is the perfect law of liberty, you discover also the biblical truth that "His commandments are not burdensome" (I John 5:3). There's no more "grinding out" the Christian life, no more complaining that it's too hard.

When you're in love, you do all you can for the one you love, not because you have to, but because you want to. That's the way it is when God works in your heart and transforms you by His truth. You fall in love with Him, you become transformed by abiding in His presence, and your one desire is to please this Lord whom you love. —:•

HAVING A RELATIONSHIP WITH GOD'S WORD

James instructs us to abide in the Word of God. The word *abide* carries with it the idea of a close relationship, such as between an infant and its mother. When an infant feeds at his mother's breast, he receives nourishment, but he's doing it in the context of a mother-child relationship.

That is the same word Jesus used when He told the disciples, "Abide in Me, and I in you. As the branch cannot bear fruit of itself unless it abides in the vine, so neither can you unless you abide in Me. I am the vine, you are the branches; he who abides in Me and I in him, he bears much fruit, for apart from Me you can do nothing" (John 15:4–5).

Our new natures have already been preprogrammed by God to feed on God's Word and respond to it, and this is in fact the only information they will respond to. It happens as we abide in Scripture, as we develop a relationship with God's Word in which we gaze into it intently and see Jesus looking back at us. When we do that, God reveals to us the things in our lives that need to change. But more important than that, His Holy Spirit empowers us to be more and more like Jesus as we look into the mirror of His Word.

James calls the Word of God "the perfect law, the law of liberty." God's written Word is absolutely perfect, absolutely inerrant in every way. But God didn't give us the Word just to give a perfect Book. He gave it to us so that we can be transformed into the image of Jesus Christ, His perfect Son.

So how do we abide in a relationship with the Word of God? We carry it with us in much the same way a woman daily carries her compact so she can look at herself at any time and make any needed changes. By that, I don't mean that you carry a Bible with you under your arm twenty-four hours a day. I mean that you make reading and meditating on the Word a part of who you are, just as you make your relationship with your spouse a part of who you are. You interface with the Word on every aspect of your life.

Read it every day. Read it chapter by chapter and topic by topic. Study God's viewpoint *first* regarding issues you are facing in your life. Read it with the attitude that says, "Lord, I give You permission to use what I read in Your Word to transform me into the image of Your Son. Reveal Yourself to me, and reveal myself as You see me."

When you do that, God through His Holy Spirit takes what you read and meditate on and empowers you to act on what you've read. He uses it to create that whole new you, one who acts, talks, and thinks like Jesus Christ.

Four

Transformed by Trials

I n the popular television show *Extreme Makeover*, people allow themselves to be put through all kinds of adversity, discomfort, and suffering so that their outward appearance can be changed for the better.

The participants of the show don't just go in for new hairstyles and wardrobes but for a complete transformation of their appearances. The processes themselves include cosmetic, plastic, and dental surgeries that not only improve how they look but change their appearance so completely that it's often difficult to even recognize the person without the "before and after" segment of the show.

Just as the participants on *Extreme Makeover* go

through a process of transformation, we as believers go through our own transformation. Ours, however, has nothing to do with our outward appearance and everything to do with inner changes. There is a similarity between these transformations, though, and it's this: both can mean discomfort and even pain.

TRIALS: CHISELS IN THE HAND OF GOD

A lot of people come to faith in Jesus Christ believing that all their problems will be solved, that they will have a life of perfect peace and harmony from that time on. Unfortunately, that is because we believers too often don't give seekers the complete story when it comes to what it means to be saved. The complete truth is that the Bible contains example after example of how men and women of God have endured terrible suffering not in spite of their faith but because of it.

I pointed out earlier that the Holy Spirit is God's agent of transformation and that the Bible, God's written Word, is the instrument He uses. But there is yet another element

God uses to transform us: adversity. The truth and the whole truth is that He not only allows adversity and suffering in the life of the believer, but sometimes even directly causes it. And why? Because adversity, when rightly handled, has a way of molding us and transforming us and making us more and more the kind of believers God wants us to be.

> When you soak a sponge in water and then press on it, what's inside comes out. But if there's no water in the sponge, you can squeeze on it all day and see nothing emerge. If nothing is soaked in, nothing will come out. Likewise, if not much spiritual reality is coming out of us when we're being squeezed by trials, it's because not much spiritual reality has ever soaked in. —:•

One of the best-known examples of this truth is found in the epistle of James: "My brethren, count it all joy when you fall into various trials, knowing that the testing of your faith produces patience" (James 1:2–3 NKJV).

As we look at what James tells us about trials, we need to take note that the apostle didn't write, "*if* you fall into various trials" but "*when* you fall into various trials." There is a premise in that statement and it's this: Trials are going to be a part of life and a part of our walk with Jesus Christ.

A "trial," as James uses the word, is not simply everyday frustrations and disappointments we all face—although those things can be part of a trial—and it's not the suffering and adversity we bring on ourselves through our own foolish decisions. A trial in this context is a divinely ordained difficulty God either causes or allows in order to chip away at our imperfections and flaws in order to make us more like Jesus Christ.

The word *various* in this passage can be translated as "multicolored," meaning that life trials can be of many kinds and come from many sources. They can be circumstantial, financial, relational, and emotional. They can hit as loneliness, discouragement, disappointment, rejection, fear, and any of countless other ways. They can hit suddenly, like a pop quiz in a college course, and they can come like major exams in that they are things we can more or less expect, plan for, and prepare for.

But what is our part in making sure that the adversity God allows or even sends our way does what He intends it to do, namely developing us spiritually? James tells us.

OUR RESPONSE TO TRIALS

God first saved us for the purpose of transforming us and conforming us to the image of Jesus Christ. We need to understand that He will not be satisfied until that happens and that He will use any means necessary to bring it about, including allowing or sending as much trouble as it takes until we respond to Him and allow Him to make the inner changes we need to become more like His Son.

James 1:2 lays for us our groundwork for responding to the trials God allows or sends, telling us, "count it all joy when you fall into various trials." In other words, when you are faced with a trial—with any kind of suffering or discomfort—you can rejoice in knowing that nothing you go through will be wasted and that God can cause it to work together for good for you "who are called according to His purpose" (Romans 8:28).

That sounds like great advice, doesn't it? But can you remember the last time you were actually filled with joy or excitement while enduring a problem or struggle? Can you remember looking at the difficulty you were going through yet choosing to give glory, honor, and praise to God right in the middle of it?

That is exactly what James tells us we are to do—to rejoice *in* a trial. But this isn't a simple command. On the contrary, he tells us that we can know the purpose for our pain, no matter how senseless and random it may seem to the outside world.

THE VALUE OF KNOWING

The late summer and early autumn of 2005 was a time when the world was witness to incredible suffering on the part of hundreds of thousands of residents in coastal

Alabama, Mississippi, Louisiana, and Texas. Hurricane Katrina, and shortly afterwards, Hurricane Rita, ripped through the Gulf Coast areas, leaving widespread death, damage, and destruction.

Like so many Americans, my heart ached for the thousands of people whose lives were turned upside-down, who had to endure the suffering these horrible storms wrought. So many survivors were left to face life after the loss of everything they had, including their loved ones.

But as difficult as it was to witness what these poor souls had to endure, I was equally grieved when I watched the news reports and heard the one question that seemed to be at the heart of everything so many survivors said in the aftermath: Why?

For the nonbeliever, adversity and suffering, particularly the kind brought about by natural disasters, can seem so arbitrary and senseless. Whether the pain is caused by a hurricane or earthquake, by an illness or injury, or by the actions of another, the one who hasn't placed his or her faith in God will almost always have a difficult time making sense of it all.

But it's not supposed to be that way for those who have placed their faith in Jesus Christ. Though in the midst of our suffering we may not know what God has in mind as He allows it, we can, in the words of the apostle James, be those, "knowing that the testing of your faith produces patience [or endurance]." In other words, when you trust God enough to know that He knows what He's doing in the midst of everything, you don't have to go through your difficulties complaining, irritable, and defeated.

There truly is no such thing in the life of a Christian as a purposeless trial, no such thing as "just having a bad day," no such thing as purposeless pain. And when we fix our minds on the fact that God has a purpose for anything we're going through, no matter how difficult it may be, we are better able to fix our eyes on what God has in mind for us and not on the difficulties themselves.

That is exactly what the apostle Peter was referring to when he wrote:

Beloved, do not be surprised at the fiery ordeal among you, which comes upon you for your testing, as though some strange thing were happening to you; but to the degree that you share the sufferings of Christ, keep on rejoicing, so that also at the revelation of His glory you may rejoice with exultation. If you are reviled for the name of Christ, you are blessed, because the Spirit of glory and of God rests on you. (1 Peter 4:12–14)

Peter knew what he was talking about. Most believers remember Peter as the apostle with foot-in-mouth disease, the one who, though he seemed to have his heart in the right place, always said the wrong thing and did the wrong thing at the wrong time. We especially remember him as the one who vowed that he would never abandon Jesus, even if it meant dying with Him (Matthew 26:35), only to deny even knowing Him as He was facing trial and execution (vv. 70–75).

But think about the post-resurrection, Spirit-filled Peter, the Peter who wouldn't stop preaching the name of Jesus Christ in Jerusalem, even in the face of threats to life and limb from the very same people who had turned Jesus over to the Romans to have Him crucified. Peter spent the remainder of his life after Jesus' death, resurrection, and ascension boldly and bravely preaching His name, even though doing so meant persecution the likes of which none of us have ever seen.

You never read of Peter saying "Why me?" as he endured these things. Instead, he pressed forward in what Jesus had called him to do, knowing that something good—namely people hearing the name of Christ—would come through his own suffering. Peter wanted his readers to know that when they were hated and persecuted on account of Jesus, they should never moan or groan about it, but instead, realize that they were not only going through God-ordained trials but were also actually partnering with Jesus in His suffering.

James calls this kind of suffering "the testing of your faith." That's a test Peter passed in spades and one God intends for all of His people to pass.

THE MEANING BEHIND THE "TESTING"

If you've ever taken tests in school, you know that it's one thing to tell an instructor that you know the material he or she has been teaching but another thing altogether to prove that you know it by taking and passing a test. Likewise, saying you trust God and are willing to follow His leading no matter where He tells you to go or what He tells you to do is very different from doing it.

A good teacher won't take our word for it when it comes to passing a test, and neither will God. That's why God allows and even causes those times of testing, why He allows our faith to be put through the fire of adversity.

James tells us that it is important to understand that God has a purpose for our suffering and that we need to be willing to allow that purpose to take its course: "And let endurance have its perfect result, so that you may be perfect and complete, lacking in nothing" (1:4).

> *Any* adverse circumstance that comes into your life is a purposeful test, because it must first pass through God's fingers. —:•

This is what we call a conditional promise. In other words, God wants us to be "perfect and complete"—conformed in the image of Jesus Christ—but that can't happen if we attempt to end the trial before God wants it ended.

Most of us when we are going through a trial want it to end yesterday. That is absolutely normal and natural simply because nobody wants or enjoys pain or problems. But God wants us to know that we are never to use illegitimate or ungodly means to get out of our trials. If you're going through a trial in your marriage, for example, you should never consider a nonbiblical grounds for divorce as a means of escape. That's because we know that it is very clear in God's Word that He hates divorce (see Malachi 2:15–17).

When it is time for us to get out of our trial, God will give us a clear exit sign, and it will always line up with what

He has to say in His written Word. And if He hasn't given you that exit sign, you can know that He is still working it out and He will eventually finish what He started when He allowed or brought that trial into your life in the first place (Philippians 1:6). In other words, if you have not yet passed the test, He will continue to use it to transform you and eventually bring you through the trial.

Some Christians have been going through the very same trial for decades simply because they haven't yet passed the test God has sent their way. That's because God is interested more than anything in bringing us to Christlikeness and spiritual maturity, and will test and retest us, then re-retest us again until we pass (see Deuteronomy 2:3).

When you go through a trial, whatever kind of trial it might be, you can know that God is bringing you into conflict with your physical realm because He wants to draw your attention to something in the spiritual realm during the conflict. Part of conforming you to the image of Jesus Christ is focusing your heart and your mind on the spiritual, on the things of God.

So it's important when we are going through a trial that we don't make the mistake of reacting to it only in the physical. We can't look at a financial difficulty as simply a financial difficulty and nothing more. Likewise, we can't look at a relational problem apart from the spiritual lessons God is trying to teach us. Though many believers have difficulty seeing it, God uses our life situations, other people, and even the devil to accomplish His divine purposes.

LEARNING TO COUNT

Who among us hasn't at some point in our lives wondered why we are suffering or what we've done to deserve it? Who among us hasn't looked at what we're going through and thought, *It's just not fair*? Sometimes when we are going through trials, life just doesn't add up. We've done nothing to bring the pain on ourselves—at least as far as we know—and it just doesn't seem fair that we should have to suffer the way we are.

That is why James, writing through the inspiration of

the Holy Spirit, tells us, "count it all joy when you fall into various trials." This is a matter of faith, a matter of taking what we don't understand—our pain—and looking at it through the spiritual lens—God's incredible love for us and His desire to transform us and make us more like Jesus.

In this passage, the word *count* is an accounting term. It suggests putting the pain and difficulty we are going through on one side of a ledger and the joy and blessing we receive in and through that pain on the other side and seeing that we are running "in the black" as far as the joy and blessing are concerned. In other words, James is telling us, "Do the math, and you'll see that you are coming out ahead, no matter what is going on in your life."

Instead of "counting it all joy," too many believers respond by complaining, arguing, fussing, and cussing. They don't count the joy in the midst of their pain but instead focus on the pain itself.

God wants us to understand that He doesn't expect us to count the pain itself as joy. He doesn't expect us to say, "I'm so happy that I'm hurting." God wants us to count the *purpose* of that pain as joy, and that purpose is to test our faith and give us endurance or, in other words, further transform us into the image of Jesus Christ.

The perfect example of counting the joy in the midst of pain is Jesus, "the author and perfecter of faith, who for the joy set before Him endured the cross, despising the shame, and has sat down at the right hand of the throne of God" (Hebrews 12:2).

Obviously there was a lot about going to the cross that Jesus wasn't going to like. He wasn't going to *like* the emotional pain of the hours leading up to that event. He wasn't going to *like* standing before earthly authorities who had no authority over Him that He didn't give them. He wasn't going to *like* being abandoned by His closest earthly friends. He wasn't going to *like* the physical pain of being brutally beaten then nailed to a cross of wood. He wasn't going to *like* the separation from His Father because He had become sin for us. That is why He prayed in all honesty, "My Father, if it is possible, let this cup pass from Me" (Matthew 26:39).

Jesus was in unspeakable pain, but He was also focused on two things. First, He was focused on doing the will of His Father, even though it meant physical and emotional pain none of us can even imagine. Second, He was focused on the joy of Sunday, when He would be gloriously raised from the dead, and not on Friday, when He would suffer all the pain of dying on the cross.

Jesus was in pain, even before He was arrested, and He didn't ignore the pain but instead went to the Father with it. God doesn't expect any of us to ignore our pain and go on like we aren't hurting. Pain hurts, and it's impossible to ignore it. But when we are going through a trial, it's vital that we change our focus from the pain itself to God's purpose for it. It is perfectly acceptable to God for us to pray something like this: "Lord, I am in pain now. And though I don't know why You have allowed this to happen to me and would rather it end now, I want to give You thanks because I know that You are going to use what's going on in my life to transform me and make me more like Your Son, Jesus Christ."

God may have you in the fire right now…but only because He wants to make sure you're "well done" for the Master. Sometimes it means that although you think you're ready, He must put you back into the fire, because He knows what you do not. And He is both the Cook, and the Master at the table.

So whatever you're going through now, count it all joy. If you've been complaining, go before God and acknowledge, "I have sinned." Ask Him to give you His perspective on this trial, and commit yourself to get into His Word to find out. Then let Him bless you from the inside out. —❖•

This is a test God wants all of His children to pass, because when we come to a point in our walk with Him where we can honestly count it all joy when we are suffering, it is proof that we have adopted the mind of Jesus Christ, that we have become more conformed to His image.

PRAY...BUT FOR THE RIGHT THING

It seems almost second nature for most people when they are enduring difficulties to do one thing: pray. That is exactly what James instructed us to do when he wrote: "But if any of you lacks wisdom, let him ask of God, who gives to all generously and without reproach, and it will be given to him" (James 1:5).

It has been said that God answers all prayers in one of three ways: "yes," "no," and "not yet." But there is a certain kind of prayer that God *may* not answer, and it's this one: "Lord, why is this happening to me?" It is human nature to want to know the "whys" of our suffering, and it's not necessarily wrong to ask God about it. But I have learned that most of the time, He doesn't answer that question, other than to let us know that He will bring something good out of it.

That brings me to the prayer that God has promised us in the Book of James that He will always answer with a resounding "Yes," and it's a prayer for wisdom. James tells us very specifically that if we don't have wisdom, we are to ask God, and He will give it to us "generously and without reproach." This literally means that we are to boldly ask God to bless us with wisdom knowing that He doesn't resent us asking.

God will always honor us when we pray and ask Him how to apply His truth as He has revealed it to us in the written Word so that we can receive the maximum spiritual blessing. But what exactly does the wisdom we are to pray for look like? In another version of the Bible, James defines wisdom as knowing what God wants us to do in our situation. In other words, God wants us to pray first about how we should respond to our trials, not about why we're suffering.

The prayer for wisdom is not a prayer for a divine explanation—because you may not get that. The prayer for wisdom is this: "Lord, in this present difficulty, how do I respond in a way that reflects how You want me to respond, so I can get the maximum spiritual benefit?"

Everyone has times in their lives when they have all the reason they need to turn to God in prayer. Unfortunately, too many of us make prayer our last resort when we are going through times of trouble. But whenever we are hurting, when we are faced with problems and trials that are too big for us to handle, our *first* move should be to get on our knees and talk to God about them—not to go for more counseling, not to seek advice from our friends, and not to just grumble and complain.

God desires to give us wisdom so that we can be conformed to the image of His Son. Our only responsibility in that equation is to ask Him in faith.

PRAYING IN FAITH

James doesn't just tell us the importance of prayer for wisdom, He also tells how to pray and how *not* to pray for wisdom: "But he must ask in faith without any doubting, for the one who doubts is like the surf of the sea, driven and tossed by the wind. For that man ought not to expect that he will receive anything from the Lord, being a double-minded man, unstable in all his ways" (James 1:6–8).

To be double-minded is to be divided in your thinking. It is to try to mix together divine reasoning and human reasoning. It is like trying to go right and left or up and down at the same time, in that it creates a very unstable situation in our lives, making us more vulnerable to attacks from the enemy and less effective in our prayer lives.

If you are trying to mix your own wisdom or the wisdom of other humans with the wisdom of God, then you are what James calls "double-minded." The only legitimate wisdom is that which comes from an application of God's truth. That is the wisdom James later calls "pure, then peaceable, gentle, reasonable, full of mercy and good fruits, unwavering, without hypocrisy" (James 3:17).

That is the kind of wisdom God wants to instill in all of His people, the kind the apostle Paul describes this way: "But he who is spiritual appraises all things, yet he himself is appraised by no one. For Who has known the mind of the Lord, That He will instruct Him? But we have the mind of Christ" (1 Corinthians 2:15–16).

When we have the "mind of Christ," when we come to a point in our spiritual growth where we are able to think like Him, then we will make the connection between the problems we are facing and God's purpose for those problems, which is our own Christlikeness.

When we come to that point in our walk of faith, we are well on our way to passing the tests God is making us take as we go through our own trials and troubles.

THE BLESSINGS OF A PASSING GRADE

If you read your Bible cover to cover, you will see the recurring principle that obedience brings God's blessing. James tells us that this applies for those who obediently and faithfully persevere during times of difficulty: "Blessed is a man who perseveres under trial; for once he has been approved, he will receive the crown of life which the Lord has promised to those who love Him" (James 1:12).

When we read the phrase "crown of life" in this verse, it's easy to assume that it refers to the rewards we receive on the other side of eternity. While the Bible promises us rewards in heaven when we persevere for Jesus Christ, I believe that James is also talking about something else. He is telling us that when we persevere through our present trials, we will receive the reward of life—that is, conformity to Jesus Christ—in this life.

We live in a time when many in the "Christian community" talk a lot about blessings. Everybody wants to be blessed, wants to claim and receive their blessing. Sadly, however, too many believers think of blessings in terms of the physical: a better job, a bigger bank account, a nicer house, and a better marriage. But while God's blessing can certainly include those things, they are not the essence of His blessing.

The true essence of God's blessing is not something we can grasp or possess physically. It is something we become, and that is being conformed to the image of Jesus Christ. That is what happens within us when we persevere, when we choose to rejoice through whatever God allows to come our way.

Trials are inevitable in this life, and while some of the agents God allows to bring trials into your life—other people or even the devil—might mean you harm, you can be assured that God will use them for good. In the words of Joseph, who lived through thirteen difficult years because of the hurtful actions of his brothers, "you meant evil against me, but God meant it for good in order to bring about this present result" (Genesis 50:20).

For us, "this present result" means conformity to Jesus Christ. And when we are going through difficult times, we can know that God has allowed them to happen in order to accomplish just that.

Five

Transformed by Temptation

I recently had a chance to visit with Indianapolis Colts Head Coach Tony Dungy. As he showed me around the Colts offices, he took me to the team's film library. In this room were films and tapes of countless professional football games as well as films and tapes of college games. Coach Dungy explained to me that the team used those films and tapes to study up on the tendencies of opponents and to take close looks at college players they were considering drafting.

Coach Dungy told me that when National Football League coaches study players on film and tape, they look at their tendencies. If you've ever watched the NFL's college draft, you hear scouting reports on individual players that use terms the ordinary football fan never thinks about. While we look at results, these scouts talk about what they call "intangibles." When it comes to a particular quarterback, most football fans focus on results—receptions, touchdowns, and yards—while these experts talk about things such as footwork, arm strength, and release points.

As I listened to Coach Dungy talk about these things, it occurred to me that there is a spiritual illustration in what he was saying. You see, the devil has "game film" on each of us. He not only knows about what we've done in the past and what we're doing now, he also knows what our tendencies are. He knows our strengths, our weaknesses, our desires, and what is most tempting to us when it comes to sin.

Satan uses all of those things in his efforts to tempt us so that he can pull us away from God. However, the Bible tells us that we can not only defeat temptation but that it can be used by God to further transform us and conform us to the image of Jesus Christ.

TEMPTATION DEFINED

Before I go on, I want to point out that it is *not* a sin to be tempted. A lot of believers fall into the trap of feeling guilty because they are tempted to sin. They somehow believe that if they were walking right with God that temptation would never be an issue and that they would think only about doing what was right in every situation.

Now how do I know that being tempted in and of itself is not a sin? Because the perfect Spirit of God would not have led Him into temptation, for then God Himself could be charged with sinning. Remember, Jesus Himself, the sinless Lamb of God, was tempted. Matthew's gospel tells us that almost immediately after Jesus was baptized, He "was led up by the Spirit into the wilderness to be tempted by the devil" (Matthew 4:1). Jesus faced some very real temptations during His time in the wilderness. The devil wanted more than anything to thwart what Jesus had come to earth to do, and he did his very best to appeal to Jesus' "human" side and get Him to turn from His real purposes.

If temptation were a sin, then Jesus would not have been "without sin," as the writer of Hebrews tells us (4:15). For Him, the temptation wasn't a sin, but instead, another hurdle He had to clear on His way to living a sinless life so that He could bring salvation and forgiveness to all of humanity.

Temptation may be simply defined as a solicitation to do evil. The temptation can come from many sources, including our own fleshly desires and from the devil himself. But one place the temptations we face will never come from is the hand of God Himself. The Bible says, "Let no one say when he is tempted, 'I am being tempted by God'; for God cannot be tempted by evil, and He Himself does not tempt anyone" (James 1:13).

But while God Himself will never tempt us, we need to understand that absolutely nothing comes into the life of the believer without God's approval. In the last chapter, I said that when we are faced with trials or difficulties, it is because God has allowed them in our lives and sometimes even caused them so that we can grow and become conformed to the image of Jesus Christ. Temptations are like trials and difficulties in that God uses them for our growth, but there is a difference in how the two come into our lives. While God may at times actually cause trials to spring up in our lives, He will never directly tempt us to sin. What He will do, however, is allow those things to come our way.

At first glance, that might seem like a bit of a contradiction, but the Bible contains some examples of God allowing temptation. We can find a good illustration of this point in the life of a well-known Old-Testament character.

The Book of Job shows us that Satan wants to use temptation to try to defeat us and that God will actually allow him to do it. Job was a man who had it going on. He was an extremely wealthy family man and well-respected. Most importantly, he was a man of God. "For there is no one like him on earth, a blameless and upright man, fearing God and turning away from evil," the Lord said of him in Job 1:8.

But when the devil heard God's praises of this man, he couldn't leave it alone. He told God that the only reason Job was faithful to God was that He had been so good to him, but "put forth Your hand now and touch all that he has; he will surely curse You to Your face" (1:11). In other words, the devil was asking God to allow him to tempt Job into sinning.

I want you to notice two things about this account. First, the devil had to go to God to seek permission to tempt Job. Second, God actually gave him that permission. God Himself didn't solicit Job to sin, but He did allow the devil to do so. From the devil's standpoint, this was going to be an opportunity to solicit a man of God to sin, but from God's standpoint it was a test: Was Job going to trust God through this trial, or was he going to curse Him?

That is the choice that faces each of us when we are tempted to sin.

WHEN TEMPTATION IS A TEST

James tells us, "Blessed is a man who perseveres under trial; for once he has been approved, he will receive the crown of life, which the Lord has promised to those who love him" (1:12). This verse marks a transition in the apostle's message to believers concerning endurance.

Verses 1 through 11 cover how we are to deal with adversity, while verses 13 through 16 cover temptation. There is, however, a common thread in this whole passage, one that makes verse 11 applicable to both topics: The devil wants to use both adversity and temptation to defeat you, while God wants to use both to make you stronger and to make you more and more like Jesus.

It is easy for us as believers to sometimes think that we would grow a lot faster in our walks with Jesus Christ if it weren't for all that temptation. But that's backwards, for a couple of reasons. It would be more accurate to say that we would be growing more if it weren't for our *choosing to give in* to those temptations, rather than allowing those temptations to be an opportunity for growth. Each and every time we are tempted, it is a God-allowed opportunity for growth, because it is an opportunity for us to choose God over the devil, and righteousness over sin.

> Every time we're tempted to take a
> vacation from God, it's an opportunity to
> do *good.* Because with any temptation,
> our ability to say yes to it is matched by
> the opportunity to say no.
>
> In fact, being tempted is absolutely
> critical to your growth. Growth means
> moving from one level to a higher one,
> and the hurdles you overcome are what
> define each higher level. →⦂

Every temptation to sin presents us with a choice, a choice between saying yes to what God wants us to do or saying yes to the temptation itself. And when God allows the devil or your own flesh to tempt you, He is doing so because He wants to see what you will choose. But I want to take that a step further by saying that God allows you to be confronted with what is wrong so that He can further develop within you a sense of what is right. If He is trying to develop within you the spiritual fruit of patience, He'll allow irritants into your life. If He is trying to develop within you godly love, then He will allow you to be faced with scenarios where it is difficult to love. And if you need to develop self-control, He will allow things to come to you that challenge your ability to say no.

That is a test as old as humanity itself.

The first two chapters of Genesis, which recount the story of creation, tell us that God planted all sorts of trees and other plants in the Garden of Eden, all of which were good for Adam and Eve to eat. He then gave them the freedom to eat from any of them with one exception: "From any tree of the garden you may eat freely; but from the tree of the knowledge of good and evil you shall not eat, for in the day that you eat from it you shall surely die" (Genesis 2:16–17).

It wasn't long before the devil came on the scene, doing what he does best: tempting people to disobey God. Satan approached the woman first and immediately began planting seeds of doubt in her mind. "Indeed, has God said, 'You shall not eat from any tree in the garden'?" Satan challenged her (Genesis 3:1).

This scene brings up some very serious questions.

Why would God put Adam and Eve in a scenario where the devil could tempt them? Why did He put the tree of the knowledge of good and evil in the garden in the first place? Why not just allow them to eat from any tree they wanted to?

This may surprise you to read this, but it's because of the nature of God's love for us. You see, God loves us in a way that gives us a choice to love and obey Him in return and to do it willingly. Like Adam and Eve, we have choices to make when it comes to temptation. We can say yes to the temptation and no to God, or we can say yes to God and grow. The bottom line for all of us is that when we choose obedience, we grow. When we choose sin, we don't.

WHEN TEMPTATION BECOMES SIN

James tells us where temptation ends and sin begins: "But each one is tempted when he is carried away and enticed by his own lust. Then when lust has conceived, it gives birth to sin; and when sin is accomplished, it brings forth death" (1:14–15).

The word *lust* is almost always thought of in terms of sexual sin, but in truth that word can have either a positive or a negative connotation. In some versions of the Bible, the word *desires* is used in place of "lust" in this verse. In the negative, the use of the word *desire* refers to wanting something that is not legitimate or wanting something that may be legitimate but wanting it in an illegitimate way.

The scene of Jesus' temptation offers a good example of the latter. Satan knew that after Jesus had fasted for forty days, He would have a legitimate desire: something to eat. Satan had an idea, and he floated it out for Jesus to hear: "If You are the Son of God, command that these stones become bread" (Matthew 4:3). Jesus had the power to do just that, and He certainly had the need at that point. The problem, however, was that Satan was trying to entice Jesus into meeting a legitimate need in an illegitimate manner—at *his* request.

The devil wants us to see some appeal in doubting the Word of God and in giving in to temptation and sinning. But what he didn't tell Eve in the Garden of Eden, and what he doesn't tell us, is that when we do the things he is tempting us to do, we are no longer living the life of freedom Jesus came to bring us. On the contrary, we are in bondage that none of us has the power to break on our own.

> With sin you can never honestly say, "The devil made me do it." At most you can say, "The devil suggested it," or "He recommended it." But sin begins with our own desire either for something illegitimate or for getting something legitimate in an illegitimate way. —◦•

Over and over in the Bible, we are warned that sin brings death. James tells us, "when sin is accomplished, it brings forth death" (1:15). In the Bible, the word *death* often refers to separation. Adam and Eve died in several ways when they disobeyed God's command that they not eat from one tree. First, and most importantly, they died spiritually because the close relationship they had enjoyed with their God was broken. Before they sinned, they walked with God in the garden, but afterwards they hid from God out of fear and shame. But that wasn't the only way they died. They also died in their relationship with one another, and with creation. They died emotionally and economically, and, eventually, they died physically.

That is why James adds this warning when he writes of temptation, sin, and death: "Do not be deceived, my beloved brethren" (James 1:16). He wants his readers to understand that the devil's job is to tempt and deceive us, to make us believe that there are no consequences for sin.

But James doesn't stop there. He goes on to give us some practical steps in overcoming sin, all of which have to do with what we focus on. When we take those steps ourselves, we will be that much closer to God's ultimate purpose for all of us: conformity to Jesus Christ.

A CHANGE IN FOCUS

One of the major mistakes many believers make is trying to get rid of sin in their lives by focusing on the sin itself. That is like going on a diet then visiting the local

McDonald's so you can see what you're not supposed to be eating.

That is partly why Jesus instructed His followers in what we call "the Lord's Prayer" to pray, "And do not lead us into temptation, but deliver us from evil" (Matthew 6:13).

At a glance, it might look like that prayer focuses on temptation and evil, but that is a backward reading of that verse. Remember, the Lord's Prayer starts out, "Our Father who is in heaven, hallowed be Your name…" (Matthew 6:9). The focus in the Lord's Prayer isn't on temptation or evil, but on whom it is addressed to: Our Father. In that prayer, there are several requests, starting with "Give us our daily bread," and they all make specific requests of God and God alone.

It is a foundational truth that to accomplish anything for God, we need our focus to be on Him. That includes beating temptation. We have victory over temptation only when we focus our attention on God, not on the temptations themselves.

If you've ever been on a commercial airliner as it encountered turbulence, you know how your pulse can quicken and your fingernails can dig into the armrest as you feel the plane being knocked around. But you relax when you hear the reassuring voice of the captain telling you that the plane had flown into some turbulence and that he was making altitude adjustments so that it could fly in smooth air. That's because your focus has been shifted away from what scared you and onto not only the captain's assurances, but on the expertise and experience he has when it comes to flying in turbulence.

The first thing James tells us to focus on when we are in the midst of temptation is the goodness of God: "Every good thing given and every perfect gift is from above, coming down from the Father of lights" (James 1:17). In this context, the word *good* refers to all the benevolent and kind acts of God on your behalf.

One of the devil's tactics when it comes to tempting us is to turn our focus away from the goodness of God. That is exactly what he did back in the garden. When Eve pointed out to him that God had warned her and Adam, "You shall not eat from it or touch it, or you will die," he answered back, "You surely shall not die! For God knows that in the day you eat from it your eyes will be opened, and you will be like God, knowing good and evil" (Genesis 3:3–5).

God had showered His goodness upon Adam and Eve, giving them the freedom to eat from any tree in the garden except one. But the devil worked to put Eve's focus on the one thing she knew she wasn't to do. In Eve's mind, the tree of the knowledge of good and evil grew bigger and bigger until she really believed she couldn't live in the garden without eating from it.

There is a choice for us when it comes to the devil's deception and temptation. When we are tempted, will we focus on that one tree in front of us that the devil wants us to believe is the only tree we need in order to be happy, or will we focus on the goodness of God and on everything He has so freely given us?

In every temptation, God wants to know: "Will you trust Me in this? Will you trust that I will cause you to grow as you yield to Me instead of yielding to the temptation? —⁘

So when you are tempted, instead of focusing on the sin that seems so appealing, try focusing on God and on His character. Focus on everything about God's character, James is telling us. And while you're at it, start with His faithfulness.

FOCUSING ON GOD'S FAITHFULNESS

James tells us something very important about God, something that's important to focus on at all times but especially during times of testing and temptation. He tells us that everything good and perfect comes from our God, "with whom there is no variation or shifting shadow" (James 1:17).

In other words, God is not only good and generous; He's also faithful and dependable in every way. No matter what we are going through—be it a trial or a temptation— we can know that God is always the same, always ready and willing to give out of His own perfection. He cannot change for the better or for the worse, and we can always count on Him in everything, including our temptations.

The apostle Paul wrote, "No temptation has overtaken you but such as is common to man; and God is faithful, who will not allow you to be tempted beyond what you are able, but with the temptation will provide the way of escape also, so that you will be able to endure it" (1 Corinthians 10:13).

When most Christians are faced with trials and temptations, they tend to begin thinking that no one has ever gone through what they're going through. But Paul wants us to know that while Satan is the master tempter, he hasn't really come up with anything very original.

I don't know about you, but I find comfort in that. But even more comforting to me is the second half of what Paul had to say about temptation: "God if faithful…" The word *faithful* in this verse is an absolute, meaning that you can always depend on God no matter what you are going through…and no matter what kind of temptation you face.

God wants us to know that if He allows a temptation to come our way, then He'll give us a way to handle it. Satan wants to put heat on us and make us turn away from God and sin, but it's our heavenly Father who has

His hand firmly on the thermostat. He decides what kind of temptations we face, how long we face them, and how intense they are.

It's pretty easy to recognize when temptation comes our way, but sometimes it's not so easy to see the way out God has promised us. That can be for one of two reasons. Either we aren't looking for it, or we just don't want to see it. We're very much like a driver traveling down the road who is so focused on the potholes that he misses the sign for the exit he was supposed to take.

It is vitally important when we are faced with temptation that we remember the faithfulness of God in everything, including providing us an escape from what tempts us. God has promised us an escape when we go through temptation, but we also need to read the second half of His promise: "that you will be able to endure it."

If you're enduring something, then you're still in the middle of it. So what is God saying when He promises us an exit? Well, it's not an exit in the sense that it always takes us completely away from the temptation (though sometimes it might). Rather, it's an exit that doesn't take us out of something, but through it. It's an exit called "endurance."

There are many examples in the Bible of God taking people out of trying situations and just in the nick of time. In His wisdom, God knew that His people had endured all they could, and it was time to deliver them. But there are just as many examples in the Word of God leaving people in those situations for a while. In either case, God's goal for those people was growth, and He never put them through more than He knew they could endure.

> Turn your focus from the sin that is tempting you, and from how problematic it is, to how faithful and loving God is. —:

FOCUSING ON GOD'S WORD

The Bible tells us that God's Word is alive and that it gives life. That is exactly what James is referring to when he wrote, "In the exercise of His will He brought us forth by the word of truth" (James 1:18).

We who were once dead in sin were made spiritually alive when we first heard and responded to the Word of God. Unfortunately, though, too many believers don't walk in the power of God's Word. For too many of us, the Bible is like the Queen of England. Yes, she holds the top position in Great Britain and, yes, she is held in high esteem. But in reality, the Queen of England has no real power. She can't pass any laws or make any meaningful proclamations.

The same can be said of the place the Bible holds in the lives of too many believers. They hold it in high esteem and acknowledge that it's God's Word, but it gives them no power when it comes to fighting off the deceptions and temptations of the devil.

The devil can handle a lot of things we throw at him, but one thing he can't take is the truth of Scripture. Jesus demonstrated that as He answered each of the devil's temptations with "It is written…" (Matthew 4:4,7,10). Jesus didn't get into a discussion with the devil over his temptations. He didn't bargain with the devil, didn't grit His teeth and say "No, I won't!" Instead, He just said, "Hey, devil, let's have a Bible study!" Satan had no answer for the truth of God's Word, and all he could do was flee the scene and scheme for another day.

Let's be logical here. If Jesus, the Living Word, needed to use the written Word to repel the devil, how much more do you and I need to use it when it comes to answering his lies, deceptions, and temptations?

There are several reasons why God the Father found it necessary to send Jesus into the wilderness so He could be tempted. One of those reasons was so that He could go on offensive against the tempter, using Scripture as His weapon of choice. That's also one of the reasons God allows the devil to tempt us. He wants us to see the power of His Word over an enemy who would love nothing more than to destroy us with his temptations.

The Bible refers to the Word of God using several terms. One of those is the Greek word *logos*, which simply means the written Word, the book we call the Bible. But there is another term for the Word of God—the word *rhema*—and it refers to God's truth spoken directly to you personally.

When you hear someone say they've received a *rhema* from God, they're saying that they've read a Scripture passage and received from the Holy Spirit personal application. When that happens, the words written in the Bible jump off the pages and become theirs personally. That is when the Word of God becomes the powerful, two-edged sword God intended it to be for us.

The devil doesn't mind you owning a Bible or even carrying it with you when you go to church. But what he doesn't like is when you take the time to know the Word and learn to use it as a weapon of offense against him. He knows that when you learn what the Word of God says to you personally, he is powerless against you because you've learned that he just can't handle the truth of Scripture.

FOCUSING ON GOD'S PLAN FOR YOU

When many believers think of the wonderful plans God has for their lives, their minds move toward this wonderful Scripture verse: "'For I know the plans that I have for you,' declares the LORD, 'plans for welfare and not for calamity to give you a future and a hope'" (Jeremiah 29:11).

That's a beautiful promise to be sure, but James also has something to say about God's plan for our lives: "In the exercise of His will He brought us forth by the word of truth, so that we would be a kind of first fruits among His creatures" (James 1:18).

The term "first fruits" is an important one in the Bible. It's an Old Testament term and a farming term God used to let His people know that He owned the first part of every harvest and that they were to bring the tithe—or the first "one-tenth"—of what they had produced.

God expected His people to bring Him their very best. The tithe couldn't be the leftover tenth. If they farmed ten acres of land, then they were not to bring God the harvest from the last acre. It had to be the "first fruits" and it had to be given before the farmer took his ninety percent. Giving any less than that was an insult to God because it devalued Him.

When the Bible tells us that we as believers are to be "a kind of first fruits among His creatures," it is saying something about the special place God holds in His heart for His own children. This tells us that God values us more than we can fully grasp, that there is nothing more important to Him than the ones who have been made whole and forgiven through Jesus Christ.

One of the reasons so many believers fail in their efforts to be more like Jesus and why so many of us don't have victory over temptation is that we don't realize how God sees us. When He sees you, He sees His "first fruits," meaning that we are to be creatures of the highest order, the cream of the crop.

The apostle Peter tells those who know Jesus Christ, "But you are a chosen race, a royal priesthood, a holy nation, a people for God's own possession" (1 Peter 2:9).

We all have at least some idea of how royalty lives. We know that kings, queens, princes, and princesses don't live in squalor, don't eat scraps from the garbage, and don't sit on street corners begging for coins. To do so would be below the dignity of a royal. If you've placed your faith in

Jesus Christ, then you're one of God's very own people, and that means you've got royal blood flowing in your veins. As such, it is beneath your dignity and your place in creation to allow Satan to tell you what to do.

Allowing the devil to make you believe that you can't make it without drugs and alcohol is below your dignity as royalty. To allow him to deceive you into thinking that you've got to make yourself feel valuable by sleeping around is below your dignity. To allow him to make you believe that you've got to engage in sin of any kind is below your dignity.

The devil wants more than anything for us to live below the dignity of one God calls royalty, and he'll do everything within his power to tempt you into living below where God has chosen you to live. But our heavenly Father has a plan for his temptations, and it's to help us to grow into beautiful reflections of the One and Only perfect man who ever walked the earth: Jesus Christ.

Six

The New You...
It's a Process

If there is one thing I want you to take away from reading this book, it's that God is passionately devoted to one goal for each and every one of His children: Christlikeness. He wants each of us as believers to be "transformed into the same image [His image] from glory to glory" (2 Corinthians 3:18) so that we can be reflections of His Son in our every word, every thought, and every action.

So passionate is He about that goal that when He saved us, He gave us everything we need to become mature, Christlike believers. Our part in that bargain is to do the simple things it takes to allow His Spirit to move in us and do the transforming.

In this book, I've talked about the tools and means God uses to transform us. I've talked about how He takes His written Word and makes it alive within us through the work of the Holy Spirit. I've talked about how He uses trials and temptations to bring us to maturity and to a higher level of Christlikeness every day we walk with Him.

Now, I want to close by telling you that this transformation is not an event but a process, one that includes the use of time, a new focus on a growing relationship with God, and spiritual development. You don't just wake up one day a spiritual adult. You can't take a pill to make it happen. You can't go to a seminar, hear a great message, or read and apply a twelve-step book and all of a sudden be made spiritually mature. You are transformed through a process in which God uses every tool at His disposal to transform us "from glory to glory."

When we are first saved, we become like fruit trees in blossom. A tree at that point in its development may look nice, but it isn't bearing fruit. But everything that tree needs—buds, then blossoms, then green fruit—to bear delicious, ready-to-eat fruit is in place and developing.

THE LOOK OF MATURITY

As you go to church, talk to other believers, and listen to the sermon, you'll hear the term "spiritual maturity" thrown around. If you were to ask most of your brothers and sisters in Christ what they want most in their walks with Jesus, they just might tell you, "I want to be more mature in Christ."

But what exactly is spiritual maturity, and what is its purpose in our lives? The apostle Paul tells us:

And He gave some as apostles, and some as prophets, and some as evangelists, and some as pastors and teachers, for the equipping of the saints for the work of service, to the building up of the body of Christ; until we all attain to the unity of the faith, and of the knowledge of the Son of God, to a mature man, to the measure of the stature which belongs to the fullness of Christ. As a result, we are no longer to be children, tossed here and there by waves and carried about by every wind of doctrine, by the trickery of men, by craftiness in deceitful scheming." (Ephesians 4:11–14)

Paul is giving us a contrast here, the contrast between children and adults. Those of us who are parents can certainly appreciate Paul's characterization of children in this passage. We know how children can be: emotionally unstable, gullible when it comes to new fads, short when it comes to their attention span, and easy to manipulate. Children want what they want *right now*, and they're prone to changing their desires from one moment to the next.

Adults, on the other hand, are usually more stable. They don't bounce from one place to the next. They are more focused and more likely to hold firmly to what they believe in. That is because they have gone through the sometimes-painful process of maturing physically, emotionally, and socially.

Paul's point in this passage is that there is a difference between spiritual "children" and "adults." And he wants us to understand that God's goal for you and me is that we become everything we were created to be: spiritually mature believers, people who have developed in their faith to a point where they consistently view and live life from God's perspective and not their own.

But, as Paul suggests in the fourth chapter of Ephesians, spiritual maturity isn't something that happens overnight.

MATURITY: IT TAKES TIME

When I was a teenaged boy, I had conflicts with my father when I wanted to do something he didn't want me to do or go someplace he didn't want me to go. When he told me no, I would protest, "But Dad, I'm almost a man!" When I said that, Dad always responded the same way: "When you become one, I'll let you know."

I hated hearing that at the time, but I now understand that my father had many things I couldn't have had at that age, starting with maturity and wisdom. He knew what was best for me, and he knew that there would come a day when I could make my own decisions about what to do and where to go.

A lot of new Christians are like a teenager who just

can't wait to be a man. They long for the day when they have been transformed into the kind of Christians who demonstrate maturity in every aspect of their spiritual lives. Sometimes, that's because they haven't been believers long enough to know that becoming a mature believer takes time, even for those who make that kind of growth their life's priority.

Ephesians 4 suggests a time element when it comes to attaining spiritual maturity as it tells us, "… for the equipping of the saints for the work of service, to the building up of the body of Christ; *until* we all attain to the unity of the faith" (vv. 12–13).

When someone uses the word *until*, it implies that there is a time equation. It is the very same word Paul used—and has the same meaning—when he wrote, "For I am confident of this very thing, that He who began a good work in you will perfect it *until* the day of Christ Jesus" (Philippians 1:6).

For those who just can't wait for a time when they reach that level of maturity, these two verses give us two wonderful promises: First, if God started it, He's going to finish it. He's not just going to save us and let it rest at that but will do everything it takes to transform us and bring us to maturity in Him. Second, they tell us that spiritual maturity isn't a destination but a process that He will continue in us from the point we accept Jesus Christ as Savior through the rest of our natural lives or until He returns.

IT TAKES TIME, BUT HOW MUCH?

The Bible makes it very clear that there can be a point in the life of every believer where he or she consistently responds to things from God's perspective. That doesn't mean absolute sinless perfection—that only comes once we're in heaven. What it means is that whatever comes our way, including our stumbles, we will respond in the way God would have us respond simply because we have the mind of Christ.

But how long does it take? How much time do most of us need to spend in the faith before we reach that level of maturity?

Well, in some ways that depends on us.

One of the things I tell people in our church membership class is that there is a simple equation when it comes to getting from where we are now to where we want to be, and it's this: Rate multiplied by time equals distance. In other words, the faster we travel toward a destination, the less time it takes us to get there. If I get in my car and head for a spot in downtown Dallas at the same time someone else starts walking for the same place, I'm going to get there a lot faster. In fact, I'll probably have had lunch, headed back home, and gone to bed by the time they get downtown.

I've seen the relevance of that illustration in people I've known who have been coming to church for years but who aren't any closer to spiritual maturity than when they first started coming. They got saved, started coming to church every time the doors were open, attended every fellowship and Bible study available—and yet they're still not downtown yet. And why? Because they're still crawling when they should have been walking or even running years ago.

God's goal for every believer is to conform us to the image of His Son, and that requires time. But that doesn't mean we are to just sit around waiting for it to happen. It requires the proper use of our time.

The question each believer needs to ask is, "What am I doing with the time God has given me to maximize my spiritual maturity?" If we are doing the basics God asks of us—such as reading His written Word and learning through the Holy Spirit to apply it to day-to-day life—then we are proactively making progress toward spiritual maturity. But if we never move beyond that first stage in our spiritual development, we can't expect God to just magically move us there.

Growing in maturity requires us to make some decisions, the most important of which is to grow in our relationship with Him.

GROWING IN A RELATIONSHIP

All too often, Christians tend to define their spiritual lives in the negative, as in what they're *not* doing—they're not drinking, they're not smoking, they're not fooling around sexually outside of marriage. In other words, they believe

they are doing well with God because they aren't doing
anything they know is wrong.

But focusing on the negative like that is backwards—
completely backwards. You see, the Christian faith isn't
about what we're *not* doing but about what we are. And
what are we to be doing? The apostle Peter tells us in his
second epistle:

> You therefore, beloved, knowing this beforehand,
> be on your guard so that you are not carried away
> by the error of unprincipled men and fall from
> your own steadfastness, but grow in the grace and
> knowledge of our Lord and Savior Jesus Christ. To
> Him be the glory, both now and to the day of eter-
> nity. Amen. (2 Peter 3:17–18)

When Peter tells us, "grow in the grace and knowledge of our Lord and Savior Jesus Christ," he is pointing
out one of the keys to being transformed through the
work of Jesus in our lives, namely that it's not about rules
and regulations, not about following the right steps. What

it *is* about is a real and growing relationship with God through Jesus Christ.

> When you try to use rules to change habits in your life—especially habits that have been there a long while—you may control that habit for a time, but the rules won't transform who you are inside. And without such a transformation, that bad habit is just waiting for the next good opportunity to express itself. —⁘

We live in a time when people love processes involving steps. You have six steps to this, eight steps to that, and twelve steps to something else. But when we reduce our faith in Christ to a set of steps, we make it out to be something mechanical and not relational. Still others want to reduce our faith into a set of rules, believing that if they obey perfectly they will see the spiritual growth they desire. That doesn't work, either. That is why Peter wrote "grow in grace," and not "grow in your knowledge and obedience of the law."

It someone were to tell me, "I'm going to grow spiritually by keeping the Ten Commandments and the rest of the Law," I'd have to answer, "You're not going to get there." That's not because there is anything wrong with God's Law. In fact, the Bible says "the Law is holy, and the commandment is holy and righteous and good" (Romans 7:12). But the Law was never meant to help you to grow or to make you a better Christian. On the contrary, it was written just to show you how bad off you are apart from the grace and mercy of God: "Is the Law sin? May it never be! On the contrary, I would not have come to know sin except through the Law; for I would not have known about coveting if the Law had not said, 'You shall not covet'" (Romans 7:7).

Spiritual maturity and growth are a matter of a personal relationship with our heavenly Father through Jesus Christ, not adherence to a set of rules. It is understanding that we need to grow in the knowledge of the fact that God has freely extended us His grace—doing for us what we don't deserve—and in a better personal knowledge of Jesus Himself.

Can you imagine what it would be like to grow up in a family where it was all rules and no relationship? If all a mother and father gave their children—and one another—was do's and don'ts without teaching them the concepts of love, forgiveness, and grace, then they would grow up completely unable to relate to others in a loving way. That is not to say that rules aren't beneficial—without a set of rules, there would be no order in that household. But families don't grow relationally through simply keeping rules. There must be an atmosphere where relationships based on love are allowed to flourish.

The New Testament repeatedly contrasts the Law and grace, and that tells us that God doesn't want us to come to Him using a programmed or legalistic approach. In fact, Paul tells us that, "by the works of the Law no flesh will be justified in His sight" (Romans 3:20).

So how can we "grow in the grace and knowledge of our Lord and Savior Jesus Christ"? It's not as complicated as you might think!

CONNECTING TO GOD

Growing in grace and the knowledge of our Savior means focusing on what God is doing in us in the midst of what we are going through. It means coming to God as a child would come to his gracious and loving Father and asking Him, "What is the connection between what's happening in my life now and You transforming me into the image of Your Son?" Even as you read this book, you should be asking Him, "What is the relationship between what I'm reading and the changes you want to make within me?"

You see, that's a relational question. It's a question that links you to your Father in a real and personal way. It's not asking God what programs He wants you to undertake, but instead, asking Him daily—maybe several times a day—what He's trying to do in you through what's going on in your everyday life. When you ask that question, you connect yourself relationally with your heavenly Father.

Jesus instructed His disciples how to have this kind of personal connection with God when He told them, "Abide in Me, and I in you. As the branch cannot bear fruit of itself, unless it abides in the vine, so neither can you, unless you abide in Me. I am the vine, you are the branches; he who abides in me and I in him, he bears much fruit, for apart from Me you can do nothing" (John 15:4–5).

What a beautiful word picture this is! It shows us how vital it is that we have a growing, intimate relationship with God through Christ. It suggests a relationship of absolute dependence, one in which we are confident and secure. And it shows us that when we make that relationship our driving force in life, we will grow into what God intended us to be all along—mature, healthy believers who can make a difference in one another's lives and in the world around us.

And, finally, it's a relationship that moves us along in our development, much like the nurturing care of two parents helps their child's progress.

MATURITY MEANS PROGRESSION

As parents, there may be nothing more wonderful and fulfilling than to watch the physical, emotional, and spiritual development of our children. When an infant is first born, he is a helpless bundle of need. But as he progresses and matures, he learns first how to crawl, and in what seems like no time at all, he is walking, talking, thinking, and functioning very much like an adult human.

You don't have to be a parent to know that a baby doesn't become an adult overnight. It takes years for what was once an infant to learn the skills it takes to function as a fully grown human being. But it takes more than time; it also takes development.

Likewise, there are stages of development in the life of a Christian as he or she grows from infancy to maturity in Christ.

The writer of the epistle to the Hebrews, which was addressed to first-century Jewish Christians, has something to say about spiritual maturity, and in chapters 5 and 6 we read of some deep theology that the Hebrew Christians just can't seem to be able to grasp. The writer explains why: "Concerning him we have much to say, and it is hard to explain, since you have become dull of hearing. For though by this time you ought to be teachers, you have need again for someone to teach you the elementary principles of the oracles of God, and you have come to need milk and not solid food" (Hebrews 5:11–12).

The phrase "dull of hearing" is one we see in other passages of the Bible, and it has nothing to do with the physical act of hearing. What it means in this text is that these believers can hear fine but don't yet have the capacity to understand.

Hebrews isn't addressed to new Christians. By the time this epistle had been written, it had been more than thirty years since Jesus had returned to His Father in heaven. They were like high school students walking into an algebra class when they haven't even fully grasped the basics of elementary arithmetic.

The writer of Hebrews points out that they had been saved long enough that they should be able to teach and disciple others but that they were in need of the "milk" of the Word of God—in other words, the very basics—before they could become teachers and disciplers: "For everyone who partakes only of milk is not accustomed to the word of righteousness, for he is an infant" (Hebrews 5:13).

What the writer is saying is that the Hebrew Christians had things backwards. They had been believers long enough that they should have been ready for the "meat" of God's Word—those things beyond the basics of salvation. Instead, they were still "baby" Christians who were feeding on the milk of the Word.

The writer of Hebrews wanted these immature believers to understand something that God wants us to understand today, namely that spiritual maturity is a guarantee for us. But "guaranteed" doesn't mean that it's automatic. There is a process that must take place, one we can compare to our progression from preschool through college graduation. It is during those first few years of school that the basics are learned—the alphabet, learning to count to 100, and so forth—and after that, it's progressively adding to that foundation of learning.

> There is no Christian who cannot become a spiritually mature believer. In that sense, spiritual maturity is guaranteed. But it isn't automatic; there's a development, an unfolding that must occur. —••

The apostle John suggests this progression in his first epistle:

> I am writing to you, little children, because your sins have been forgiven you for His name's sake. I am writing to you, fathers, because you know Him who has been from the beginning. I am writing to you, young men, because you have overcome the evil one. I have written to you, children, because you know the Father. I have written to you, fathers, because you know Him who has been from the beginning. I have written to you, young men, because you are strong, and the word of God abides in you, and you have overcome the evil one. (1 John 2:12–14)

There are three stages of spiritual development suggested in this passage. Stage one is that of childhood, which is when one first realizes that their sins have been forgiven through Jesus Christ. Stage two is that of youth, which is when believers begin to understand how to use Scripture to fight the temptations and deceptions of the devil. Stage three is that of fatherhood. Two things mark the father. First, he is one who knows God well, and that's because he has walked with Him through the battles of childhood and youth. Having come through those battles, he knows that Jesus is more than enough and more than able to overcome on his behalf. Secondly, being a father, he is one who reproduces in the lives of others what he has learned and experienced for himself.

WHAT'S MISSING—PROGRESS!

Sadly, there are too many believers who have been saved for twenty or thirty years or more, and they still haven't become a "father" to anyone. They've not led anyone to Jesus and haven't influenced anyone to grow in their faith. In other words, they haven't born any fruit.

The problem with believers such as these isn't a lack of God-supplied resources but a lack of development. They are still underdeveloped, weak Christians. But why is that? What is missing? It's the same problem as the one the writer of Hebrews was addressing. They have access to

God's Word, but they are still "dull of hearing." Or, to put it another way, they are still in the classroom when they should be out there living out the principles they had learned in a real-life setting.

> Spiritual growth takes place on the playing field of life, not in some classroom. —:•

God wants all of His children to continually and cease-lessly make progress in their lives of faith, and He wants that to happen from the moment they receive Christ as their Savior until the moment they leave this earth and graduate to heaven. He wants us to be models of the kind of believers the writer of Hebrews was talking about when he wrote: "But solid food is for the mature, who because of practice have their senses trained to discern good and evil" (Hebrews 5:14).

Sadly, too many Christians never make the connection between the truths of God's Word and "real life." They never graduate from the "milk" of learning biblical truths about their faith to the "meat" of actually living it in a practical, spiritually oriented way.

Part of the process of spiritual maturity is spending time in the classroom of reading our Bibles, going to church, and attending Bible studies. But growth doesn't take place in the classroom—that is where you get all the information you need to grow spiritually. Real spiritual growth takes place as you live your life. It takes place as you learn to put into practice the truths you learned in class.

That is what the writer of Hebrews was talking about when he wrote, "Therefore leaving the elementary teaching about the Christ, let us press on to maturity, not laying again a foundation of repentance from dead works and of faith toward God" (Hebrews 6:1).

When we do the things that help us to progress in our faith, we put ourselves in position to be spiritual "fathers" to others. That happens because of one thing: You have become more like Jesus in everything you do and say.

THE RESULT: CHRIST FORMED IN YOU!

Any time you go through any kind of process, it is with the goal of seeing results. That includes the process of spiritual maturity. In his letter to the Galatian church, the apostle Paul tells us what the result of going through the process of spiritual maturity is: "My children, with whom I am again in labor *until Christ is formed in you*" (Galatians 4:19).

Again, Paul uses a word picture of pregnancy and birth to help us understand what God wants to do in us. When an unborn baby is forming inside its mother, the process of pregnancy brings changes in the body of the mother—first ones on the inside that we can't see, then ones that are outwardly visible. There are internal chemical and biological changes, all of which lead to changes in the mother. Her moods change, her appetites in food and drink change, and her focus changes. Later, her belly grows bigger as the baby inside grows.

We saw earlier that when a pregnant woman's body starts changing, it's not as a result of anything she is willfully doing. Those changes began with an act of intimacy that led to this new life. She can't make herself change any more than she can keep herself from changing. She's not changing because of any program or seminar, but only because it is a natural part of being pregnant. All she can do when it comes to these changes is the things she knows are good for her and for the baby inside her and not do the things that aren't good for either. She merely cooperates externally with what is happening internally.

> "Work out your salvation with fear and trembling; for it is God who works in you…" (Philippians 2:12–13 NIV). God makes maturity possible, but *you must work it out.* He will not do it automatically. It's part of your development. There's no growth if you don't work it out. —❖

When we first come to Jesus Christ for salvation, God begins a process inside of transforming us into His image. And at the heart of the transformation is, in the words of the writer of Hebrews, our moving from the "milk" of His Word to the "meat." You see, the milk is the information about God contained in the pages of Scripture. The meat, on the other hand, is when that Word is applied, making it experiential. When that happens, we begin seeing and living life from a spiritual perspective and not a human one.

I love how the apostle Paul put it: "but just as it is written, 'Things which eye has not seen and ear has not heard, and which have not entered the heart of man, all that God has prepared for those who love Him.' For to us God revealed them through the Spirit; for the Spirit searches all things, even the depths of God" (1 Corinthians 2:9–10).

When we become spiritually mature, we experience the mind of Christ, and we are able to see things, hear things, and perceive things that those who don't know Him cannot. In other words, we begin to live in the heavenly and not in the earthly.

God wants us to understand that nothing He puts us through—whether it seems pleasant or unpleasant at the time—is without the purpose of taking us through the process of birthing from within us the likeness of Jesus Christ. That is the inner result of intimacy with God.

A Guide to Study, Discussion, and Application

QUESTIONS FOR CHAPTER 1—GOD'S ASSIGNMENT FOR US

1. In this book's title, what does that phrase *a whole new you* really mean for you?

2. What are your hopes and expectations regarding what you'll obtain or achieve from reading this book?

3. What is it about yourself or your life that you most *want* to change? What do you want to be *new*?

THE WRONG FOCUS

4. In what incidents or experiences in your life have you found yourself mistakenly seeking the wrong purpose or goal or assignment?

5. What are some of the ways you've worked hardest at being a Christian?

FINDING THE PURPOSE

6. In what circumstances or events or time periods (if any) have you ever felt that your life wasn't working out for good?

7. From your own understanding of the Scriptures, what *is* God's purpose for us? How would you express it in your own words?

8. How would you state this purpose in a personal way, just for *you?*

JUST LIKE JESUS

9. Why is it so easy for us to forget God's purpose for our lives?

10. At what times and in what ways have you been most likely to forget God's purpose for your life?

11. The Lord wants us to have a share in His glory (John 17:22,24)—a fact that has staggering, eternal implications. How can this become a priority in your life *today?*

IT'S NOT ABOUT HAPPINESS

12. In the way you normally live your life day by day, how would you rank these goals in their actual priority for you?

    ___ having a good job
    ___ having good health
    ___ your family's welfare and harmony
    ___ your personal happiness
    ___ Christlikeness

13. Do you agree that our happiness is *not* God's major objective for Christians? Why or why not?

14. In what ways can you see that you truly are becoming more conformed to the image of God's Son?

15. In what areas of your life do you feel it's hardest for you to become more conformed to the image of God's Son?

A PROBLEM OF CAPACITY

16. Have you experienced frustration or discouragement in your Christian life? If so, what seems to trigger it?

17. How would you answer this question: Why are so many Christians living in defeat when Jesus promised them victory?

18. How can we actually rely on God's Spirit living within us to "fix" the sin problems in our lives? What does this reliance involve?

19. With the Holy Spirit inside us, each of us is a candidate for a miracle every day—the miracle of resurrection. It means

a new dimension of spiritual aliveness. What encouragement does this promise from Scripture give you?

20. Do you want to be merely "a better person," or "a completely new person"? What is your true desire and expectation?

21. Christlikeness means the Spirit-inspired ability to increasingly imitate the character and conduct of Christ in and through our own bodies. Are you committed to pursuing exactly this?

Scripture passages to explore:
> Romans 13:14
> Ephesians 4:23–24
> Philippians 3:20–21
> Colossians 3:9–11
> 1 John 3:2–3

In prayer: Express fully to God your desire to experience conformity to Christ.

QUESTIONS FOR CHAPTER 2—THE ROAD TO TRANSFORMATION

1. What does it mean for something to be "natural" to you—what does that involve, and what does that exclude?

A (SUPER)NATURAL TRANSFORMATION

2. How ready are you to fully trust God to bring into *your* life a transformation to Christlikeness?

3. If God's Holy Spirit is ultimately responsible for our transformation into Christlikeness, what is our responsibility?

THE AGENT OF TRANSFORMATION

4. How much better do you think your Christian life would go if Jesus were physically present in this world today?

5. The liberty we have in the Holy Spirit means freedom from being what you once were, and freedom to be a reflection of Jesus Christ, just as God intended. How much of this true freedom are you currently experiencing?

6. What is really *new* in your life today? What *changes* are happening because of God's work in your life?

A NEW WAY OF THINKING

7. What is a good example of how you can set your mind on the things of the Spirit, as we're told to do in Romans 8:5–6?

8. What are some of the most important ways in which God's way of thinking is different from your own?

9. When we fall into sin, it never "just happens." In your own life, how have you noticed that wrong actions are rooted in wrong thinking?

10. How is it possible for Christians to still be in bondage to the flesh, even though they desire to be free?

A NEW WAY OF "LOOKING" AT GOD

11. What does it mean to you to "gaze intently at God"? How do you think this can happen in a practical way?

12. In what ways (if any) do you ever find yourself holding back from being vulnerable and exposed and fully honest with God?

KEEPING IT REAL WITH GOD

13. Is there anything in your life that you specifically do *not* want to talk with God about?

14. What are some possible examples of things that God already knows about you, though you might pretend as if He doesn't?

15. Have you given the Holy Spirit permission to change what needs to be changed in your life? In what specific areas of your life do you need to do this?

16. How do you think gazing more intently at the Lord can help you to be more honest and open with Him?

DOING WHAT'S NATURAL

17. Why is it necessary to look to God to discover what's really "natural" for you, instead of looking to your own desires and habits?

18. Are you letting God see you as you really are? What should this mean in the way you pray?

TRANSFORMED BY GAZING

19. In what ways have you been "foolish" and "slow of heart" to believe God's Word (just as the disciples were—Luke 24:25–26)?

20. Imagine yourself being present in that story from Luke 24 where Jesus walked with two disciples on the road to Emmaus. Place yourself with them at their journey's end, as they sit across the table from Jesus, and He breaks bread before them. In that moment, what do you think would impress you most about Jesus?

21. As you become better acquainted with the Lord God— as you "gaze intently" at Him—what do you expect to learn more deeply about Him? What do you *want* to learn more deeply about Him? And what difference do you want it to make in your life?

Scripture passages to explore:
>   Romans 8:2
>   Romans 8:15
>   Romans 12:2
>   2 Corinthians 4:6
>   2 Corinthians 5:17
>   Hebrews 4:15
>   1 John 3:20

In prayer: Focus deliberately in prayer on opening yourself to God honestly and transparently, exposing everything to Him—every weakness, every sin, every need.

QUESTIONS FOR CHAPTER 3—TRANSFORMED BY THE WORD

1. What obstacles or temptations are mostly likely to keep you from "eating" God's Word when you need a meal of spiritual nourishment?

2. How is the Bible like a mirror to you? What kinds of things does it show you about yourself? What kinds of things does it show you most often about the Lord?

3. Do you agree that we should expect to always be changed when we look properly into God's Word? Why or why not?

LEARNING TO "BEHOLD" GOD'S WORD

4. In what ways do you find yourself satisfied with merely being enlightened or educated by God's Word, rather than being truly transformed by it?

TIME TO LISTEN UP!

5. How often is it true that you're more interested in speaking your mind and asserting your right to be heard than you are in hearing what others have to say?

6. What does it mean to be "quick to hear" God's Word? What kind of "quickness" is needed in the way you approach the Scriptures?

7. Are the Scriptures truly *the only absolute truth* you turn to when you're seeking significant answers for your own life or for others you love?

8. In what kinds of situations do you tend to listen more quickly to human reasoning and wisdom than to God's truth as revealed in the Bible?

9. How have you recognized and cultivated the inward, instinctive craving you have for the Word of God (as a result of the Spirit's presence within you)?

READ, BUT LOSE THE ANGER FIRST

10. Have you ever found yourself being angry with God? What caused this anger? In that situation, how were you failing to be humble and reverent before Him?

RECEIVING THE WORD

11. How warm is the welcome you've given to the Word of God in your life?

12. When you genuinely acknowledged Christ as your personal Lord and Savior, the reality of God's light and truth was implanted deeply within you. How strongly

have you embraced this reality in how you think about yourself and your life?

RECEIVING WITH A READY HEART

13. What kind of sins are you most in danger of harboring in your life?

14. What particular sins and imperfections in your life is God bringing to your attention, so that you and He can deal with them?

15. What sins are most likely to be "pet sins" in your life?

16. What sins in your life do you desire to be cleansed and freed from?

17. What sin or sins do you need to confess to God at this time?

RECEIVING GOD'S WORD IN HUMILITY

18. How would you evaluate the degree of your humility in accepting the authority of God's Word in your life?

19. What do you believe are the most important issues involved in submitting ourselves to the Bible's authority?

THE IMPORTANCE OF "DOING"

20. Do you have a consistent habit of actively and obediently applying the Word of God whenever you're exposed to it? If not, why is this habit lacking in your life?

21. Whenever you *decide* to obey God's Word, the Holy Spirit will enable and empower you to turn that decision into action. How have you seen this to be true in your own life?

SEEING YOURSELF IN THE MIRROR OF SCRIPTURE

22. Why is prayer and meditation such an important part of truly understanding the Scriptures?

23. What helps you most to approach the Bible in a prayerful, meditative way?

HAVING A RELATIONSHIP WITH GOD'S WORD

24. What does that biblical word *abide* mean to you?

25. How would you describe your current "relationship" with God's Word? Is it healthy and happy?

26. Is the Word of God really a part of who you are?

27. Are there any areas or aspects of your life in which you have not fully interfaced with what the Word of God says?

Scripture passages to explore:
>Psalm 19:7–10
>Psalm 119:45
>Psalm 119:97
>John 8:31–32
>John 8:36
>John 15:10

Romans 7:12
1 John 2:24

In prayer: Express to God the kind of relationship you want
to have with His Word—how you want Him to speak
to you and to change you as you read and hear and
meditate on the Scriptures.

QUESTIONS FOR CHAPTER 4—TRANSFORMED BY TRIALS

1. In what ways are you in need of an "extreme makeover"
   in your life?

TRIALS: CHISELS IN THE HAND OF GOD

2. Have you ever, in some form or another, had the notion
   that your faith in Christ would keep you from experiencing severe adversities? If so, what was it that gave
   you this impression?

3. Why do we actually *need* adversities in our lives?

4. How hard is it for you to believe and accept that God
   not only allows adversity and suffering in our lives, but
   sometimes even directly causes it?

5. Which of the following adversities tend to be the most
   difficult for you to handle? (Or could it be something
   that isn't on this list?)

___ financial problems
___ health problems
___ disagreements in your family
___ problems with close friends
___ problems with neighbors
___ problems with people at church
___ problems with a boss or co-workers
___ too much work to do
___ discouragement
___ rejection from others
___ loneliness
___ fear

OUR RESPONSE TO TRIALS

6. When an unexpected hardship or problem suddenly arises in your life, what is your typical reaction?

7. What is the real reason that we can "count it all joy" when we encounter various trials and troubles?

8. Why is it so hard for us to rejoice in a trial in the way that God's Word commands us to do?

THE VALUE OF *KNOWING*

9. When you face hardship and suffering, how difficult is it for you to believe that God knows what He's doing in allowing those circumstances into your life?

10. What instances of suffering or trial in others' lives have been caused by your own actions?

11. What is the real reason that we can endure hardships and suffering without complaining or feeling defeated?

12. Do you agree that there is no such thing in the life of a Christian as a purposeless trial? Why or why not?

13. In what tough circumstances in life have you found yourself asking, "Why me?"

14. To you, what does it mean to be a sharer with Jesus in His sufferings (Philippians 3:10, 1 Peter 4:13)?

THE MEANING BEHIND THE "TESTING"

15. As you look back on the biggest trials and troubles you've experienced in your life, which ones would you say were tests from God that you "passed"? Which ones were tests from God that you "failed"?

16. What particular qualities does God want to build into your life as a result of the difficulties and hardships He's allowing you to go through?

17. How strongly present in your life is the virtue of patient endurance?

LEARNING TO COUNT

18. "It's just not fair"—when have you had that reaction to some struggle you were facing?

19. Why is faith so important when we face some affliction that we can't understand?

20. When you face an affliction, how strong is your tendency to focus on the pain? What can help you *not* to focus on the pain?

21. What is the real *purpose* behind the pain God brings into your life?

22. What impresses you about the way Jesus handled the pain and suffering in His life?

PRAY...BUT FOR THE RIGHT THING

23. When might it be wrong to ask God "Why?" about the suffering we're going through? When might it be right?

24. What does *wisdom* mean to you? What do you think it means to God? How often do you ask God for it?

PRAYING IN FAITH

25. What does it mean to ask God *in faith* for wisdom?

26. In what current circumstances in your life do you need to ask God, in faith, for His wisdom?

27. What does "having the mind of Christ" mean to you?

THE BLESSINGS OF A PASSING GRADE

28. How good are you at persevering under trial?

29. What has God taught you about perseverance?

Scripture passages to explore:
>Matthew 5:10–12
>Romans 8:16–17
>2 Corinthians 1:5
>Philippians 1:29
>2 Timothy 2:11–13
>Revelation 2:10

In prayer: Offer God praise and thanksgiving for His willingness and faithfulness to bring trials into your life for your good.

QUESTIONS FOR CHAPTER 5—TRANSFORMED BY TEMPTATION

1. What temptations do you tend to be most susceptible to?

2. In what circumstances is it hardest for you to resist temptation?

TEMPTATION DEFINED·

3. Why is it *not* a sin to be tempted?

4. What specific temptations did Jesus face? (See Matthew 4:1–11) Why do you think the devil brought these particular temptations to Him?

5. Why does God sometimes allow His children to be tempted by the devil?

6. In every temptation, what fundamental choice is facing us?

WHEN TEMPTATION IS A TEST

7. In all temptations and trials that we meet, what is the devil's purpose? And what is God's purpose?

8. What opportunity is God giving us in every temptation?

9. Think about the kinds of temptations you generally face. What does this say about the qualities God wants to develop in your life at this time?

10. Why is every sinful choice also a choice *not* to grow spiritually?

WHEN TEMPTATION BECOMES SIN

11. What are the strongest sinful desires that you face?

12. What legitimate needs are you tempted to meet in an illegitimate manner?

13. Think about the sins that you're most often tempted to commit. How well do you understand their harmful consequences? What are those consequences?

A CHANGE IN FOCUS

14. Beating temptation requires a focus on God. What can you do to help focus your mind on God when you face a typical temptation?

15. Spend a few moments thinking about the goodness of God and the richness of His blessings toward you. What proof of His goodness have you seen? What particular blessings from Him are you experiencing at this very moment? How does this focus help you in battling your desire for sinful things?

FOCUSING ON GOD'S FAITHFULNESS

16. Spend a few moments thinking about the faithfulness of God. What proof of His faithfulness have you seen in your life? How has He fulfilled His promises to you? How dependable have you found Him to be? And how does this focus help you in battling temptation?

17. When you've faced temptation, what "ways of escape" (1 Corinthians 10:13) have you seen God offer you, so that you can endure it?

18. Why is endurance so important in our lives?

FOCUSING ON GOD'S WORD

19. How have you seen the true *power* of God's Word in facing temptation?

20. Think about God's Word being your offensive weapon in the battle against sin and temptation. How well trained are you in using this effective weapon? Do you need more training? If so, how can you get it?

21. In recent days, what has God spoken about to you *personally*, from His Word?

FOCUSING ON GOD'S PLAN FOR YOU

22. What convinces you that God highly values you?

23. What truly convinces you that God has a plan for your life, to give you a future and a hope?

Scripture passages to explore:

> 1 Corinthians 1:9
> 1 Thessalonians 5:23–24
> 2 Thessalonians 3:3
> 2 Peter 2:9
> Jude 24–25

In prayer: Acknowledge before God the great worth of what He wants to accomplish in your life by having you face and overcome temptation.

QUESTIONS FOR CHAPTER 6—THE NEW YOU...IT'S A PROCESS

1. How have you already seen real growth and development in your Christian life?

THE LOOK OF MATURITY

2. To the best of your understanding, what *is* spiritual maturity?

3. What does God expect from those who are spiritually mature?

4. How have you grown in viewing your life more clearly from God's perspective?

MATURITY: IT TAKES TIME

5. In what ways do you ever get impatient about the pace of your spiritual growth?

6. What God starts, He finishes. What has He started in your life?

IT TAKES TIME, BUT HOW MUCH?

7. To maximize your spiritual maturity, what are you now doing with the time God has given you?

8. How would you evaluate your level of commitment toward growing in spiritual maturity?

GROWING IN A RELATIONSHIP

9. What positive *actions* in your life are a demonstration of your spiritual maturity?

10. How have you grown in receiving God's grace? How do you want to grow more in this?

CONNECTING TO GOD

11. Think about the most important things you're going through in your life right now. How do you see God's involvement in all this?

12. What is the connection between (a) what's happening in your life now, and (b) how God is transforming you into the image of His Son?

13. What increased intimacy with God have you recently experienced?

MATURITY MEANS PROGRESSION

14. Are you ready for the spiritual "meat" of God's Word, the "solid food"? Or do you still need "milk," spiritually speaking?

15. Look at the three stages of Christian maturity suggested by the words in 1 John 2:12–14. In what stage are you?

WHAT'S MISSING—PROGRESS!

16. How actively are you exercising your spirituality in real life in the real world?

17. How are you becoming a spiritual "parent" to other believers?

THE RESULT: CHRIST FORMED IN YOU!

18. How can you see that Christ truly is being formed in you?

Scripture passages to explore:

> 1 Corinthians 3:1–3
> 1 Corinthians 14:20
> Colossians 3:16
> 1 Peter 4:10–11

In prayer: Give thanks to God for the spiritual growth and progress He has already accomplished in your life, as well as for the progress He promises in your future. Talk with Him also about the areas in your life where you know He now wants to work and change.

It's About Transformation!

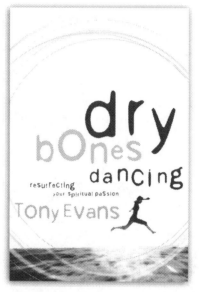

*G*od's Spirit once took the prophet Ezekiel to a vast valley filled with brittle, parched-dry bones—a potent picture of widespread spiritual dryness. But by the Word of God proclaimed through Ezekiel's mouth, those piles of bones took on sinew and flesh and skin, then were infused with life-giving, wind-driven breath from the Spirit of God. A sweeping vista of skeletons was turned instead into a force of fired-up warriors ready to do battle for the Lord. A transformation just as dramatic is what God wants to generate in our individual lives today and in the life of His church.

Dry Bones Dancing is about escaping religious dryness to move on to true spiritual passion. The results will be an experience of supernatural power and peace in the presence of God as you are invited to go deeper and see God's character and glory as never before.

When the Hits Just Keep on Comin'

*T*here are small hits: The car won't start. You lose something valuable. It's raining on your five-hundred-person outdoor event. And there are big hits: She's diagnosed with cancer. You're being laid off. They're getting divorced. Regardless of magnitude, each trial causes us to ask, "Lord, do you really care?" Tony Evans bases his resounding, "Yes, He does!" on a thorough analysis of John 11. While interacting with Martha and Mary, who were reeling from news of their brother's death, Jesus' words and actions have much to say to us today. Before, during, or after you're assaulted by doubt, pain, confusion, disappointment, or grief, this powerful book will help you zero in on Christ to ensure that no crisis of any kind will ever shipwreck your faith.

Printed in the United States
by Baker & Taylor Publisher Services